The Search for Fulfillment

The Search for Fulfillment

Revolutionary New Research
That Reveals the Secret
to Long-term Happiness

Susan Krauss Whitbourne

Ballantine Books
New York

Published in the United States by Ballantine Books, an imprint of
The Random House Publishing Group,
a division of Random House, Inc., New York

BALLANTINE and colophon are registered trademarks of Random House, Inc.

LIBRARY OF CONGRESS CATALOGING-IN-PUBLICATION DATA

Whitbourne, Susan Krauss.
The search for fulfillment: revolutionary new research that reveals
the secret to long-term happiness / Susan Krauss Whitbourne.
p.   cm.
ISBN 978-0-345-49999-8
eBook ISBN 978-0-345-51483-7
1. Happiness.   2. Self-actualization (Psychology).
3. Success—Psychological aspects.   I. Title.
BF575.H27W47 2010
155.2'5—dc22   2009036967

Printed in the United States of America on acid-free paper

www.ballantinebooks.com

2 4 6 8 9 7 5 3 1

First Edition

Book design by Drew Stevens

Contents

Author's Note

In presenting the findings from this study I have adhered to the ethical principles involved in the conduct of research with human subjects by ensuring that the confidentiality of each participant has been maintained. Therefore, I have changed all identifiable characteristics of each participant whose story is described in the book. In some instances, where gender was not a relevant factor, I changed men to women and vice versa. In other cases I altered the marital histories of participants, changed the number and gender of their children, and switched their occupations to ones that were comparable in social class, income, and relevance. I also used data from multiple participants to create compilations that represent bits and pieces from each of their life events. However, at all times I maintained the integrity of the personality data and did not change the description of scores or items that participants endorsed. The result is that the data presented here is true to the study's main findings while protecting the rights of my participants by disguising their identities. This protection is vital to any research in which life history data forms the essence of the analysis.

I would also like to note that the narrative stories included in this book stitch together the facts about the participants' lives (disguised, of course) based on my hypotheses about what happened to them at particular moments in their lives or what may happen to them in the future. These interpretations are based on my clinical training and my years of experience working with patients. My interpretive skills enabled me to analyze the patterns of their scores and life events, and to develop a narrative or "life story" based on the similar trajectories of several of the participants' lives. These stories are told as a way to illustrate and personalize the scores and responses that I received from the subjects and, in some cases, details were added for color so that readers could better relate to their experiences.

Furthermore, all students and colleagues who have worked with me in preparing data for the analyses presented in this book and in my scientific articles received training in the ethical treatment of human subjects as set forth by my university's institutional review board. They (and I) were required to pass a test to verify our credentials. An additional requirement that I have fulfilled is that I have kept the materials from the study under actual and virtual (i.e., password protected) lock and key. When asked to participate in the study, the people in my sample were informed that they were under no obligation to complete the questionnaires, and that their participation was entirely voluntary. I described the risks and benefits of being in the study, and they agreed to these conditions.

All data was collected from the group as a whole. As is customary, participants signed consent forms, as required by the institutional review board, in which they agreed to participate as long as the confidentiality of the data was maintained. In my published articles I presented the data in terms of group averages and correlations so that individuals were never identifiable by their patterns of scores. In this book, though I focus on individuals, it is not possible to connect these scores to details about their individual lives.

I am extremely appreciative for the candor with which my participants responded to questions about themselves and I look forward to following up with them very soon. Research on human development relies on the willingness of many thousands of individuals to allow psychologists to peer into their lives from time to time. The generosity of my particular sample in sharing their lives with me will, I hope, be rewarded by the knowledge that they are helping others to find their own paths to fulfillment.

Introduction

As a twenty-five-year-old assistant professor of psychology, I found my-self in the peculiar situation of teaching a course on the subject of aging. In the middle of my lecture one day, I had an "aha" moment about my own life when I realized that I was in a relationship that I very likely would regret when I got older. It was a scary feeling. But as a result, I made some changes pretty fast—perhaps too rashly—but ultimately they were the right decisions. It may sound drastic, but this single experience taught me a valuable lesson: Live your life when you're young as if you were looking back on it when you're old.

Evaluating how the choices we make now will affect us in the years to come is a complicated and difficult endeavor. My interest in how people develop goes back as far as I can remember. I am constantly looking at others through the lens of time: How will this student be when he's older? What was this new acquaintance like when she was younger?

Fortuitously, around that same time when I made my radical move as a young adult, I became enthralled by the theories of Erik Erik-son, a psychologist who believed that adults continue to develop and grow across their lifespan, that personality is not set in stone once one turns eighteen. I soon found my mission within my field: to test Erik-son's theory by studying people over time and actually mapping out how they change, to discover how their early decisions shape their en-tire lives.

My deeper, underlying motivation in wanting to find support for

Erikson's theory was my belief that people can find fulfillment at any age, that they are not stuck on predetermined paths. When I began the study on which this book is based, I wondered whether college students' scores on psychological tests (which measured feelings of fulfillment as well as personality traits and biographical details) would remain consistent if I were able to have the subjects take the test again a decade later. Would those who had been successful in college show stable patterns in their work and family lives? Would men and women differ in their patterns of fulfillment? At first, I didn't think I would pursue the study past that first follow-up. But after several years went by, I decided to continue tracking the same people over time, and now I have forty years' worth of data on the same 182 subjects.

In 1966, with dreams of changing the world, this group began their freshman year at a private college in the Northeast. After graduation, they embarked on amazingly disparate paths to become everything from international financiers to homeless drug addicts. What is perhaps more remarkable, however, is that their outward signs of success—wealth, career advancement, family cohesion—did not necessarily correlate with their internal feelings of happiness and satisfaction. Some of the happiest had not achieved what the outside world would consider real success, while some of the most powerful felt their lives were empty.

Another noteworthy result was seeing before my eyes how wrong we are to have pessimistic views of aging that say we are fated to lose our abilities and our vitality as we get older. I myself have never liked being pigeonholed. When Gail Sheehy's book *Passages* came out, I was irritated by the notion therein that we can all be pegged on the basis of our age. I'm happy to report that my research confirmed my hunch that middle-aged people are not a bunch of eternal youth-seekers in crisis. Not only can we control—to some extent—the manner in which we age, we can enjoy it.

We've all heard stories of people finding meaning later in life and making changes for the better in middle age, but this is the first time that a large-scale research study reveals how anyone can feel fulfilled, can create a sense of meaning, and, essentially, can find happiness—no matter what their level of satisfaction was in their youth.

Researchers who carry out long-term studies such as mine get a little obsessed with their work. It's like reading a great mystery, one that takes not a day, a week, or a month, but a lifetime to unfold. And it's a lifetime in which your own development becomes entwined with that of the people you observe. The people I studied were slightly older than I, close to my brother's age. I've often felt like a little sister trailing behind them, seeing my own struggles and triumphs reflected in theirs. I started my family around the same time many of them did, began my career at about the same time, and was affected by the same historical events—the women's movement, the civil rights movement, and the many changes in world politics.

Now I'd like to share with you what I've learned from analyzing all I know about the development of these people over the past forty years. I hope this book will provide a mirror for fellow baby boomers to look into, and provide a guide on how to keep developing and changing for the better at any age.

The Search for
Fulfillment

CHAPTER 1

Grown-ups and Growth

As she sifts through the day's emails, Barbara pauses to glance at the picture on her desk of her husband and children, taken on a family vacation many years ago when the children were young. Barbara shudders to think about how long ago those days now seem. More often than she cares to acknowledge, she also feels pangs of guilt when she considers the relatively few times she was able to forget about work as her children were growing up and to truly enjoy her family. Were the sacrifices she made for her career really worth her current regret?

Back in her college days, Barbara—now one of the country's leading aeronautical engineers—decided to focus her energies exclusively on work in her professor's research lab. By the time she was a senior, she had spent two summers training at the premier engineering facility in the country. Her friends and family couldn't understand why Barbara was interested in spending all her free time stuck inside a lab instead of outside enjoying the beach or just relaxing.

Barbara's hard work in college paid off, though. In her senior year, while her peers struggled to find employment or entry into a graduate degree program, Barbara was looking at several offers from the top research universities in the country, all of which promised a healthy stipend. Grad school proved to require an intense commitment, but she didn't mind the long hours. Once again, her hard work paid off: Even before finishing her degree, she had major companies bidding to employ her. Though she relished the work itself, she occasionally found herself stymied by a man, often a supervisor, who seemed to resent her meteoric rise to the top of her field.

Barbara's difficulties with men also spilled over into her romantic life. In a pattern that would repeat itself over the upcoming decade, Barbara had a tough time maintaining a steady relationship. She would become involved romantically with men only to find that they didn't understand or support her strong ambitions.

Finally, she met and married William, a man who takes his career seriously but doesn't focus exclusively on it. William doesn't seem to mind Barbara's long hours, her preoccupation, her writing and rewriting of technical plans. Yes, Barbara has finally met the man who is not only her intellectual equal but also the first man who has really understood what makes her tick.

Still, Barbara is filled with self-doubts. Despite a significant record of technical accomplishments and innovations, she's scarred from some colleagues' resentment of her pioneering success. And while she appears to have it all—a stimulating job, a beautiful home, a loving husband, and two well-adjusted children, she still wonders: Why am I not happier? Barbara knows that she's been tough to live with, and now she is beginning to see, perhaps for the first time in her life, just how tough she has been. This is probably a good realization, but it will not necessarily help her dismiss her feelings of regret and despair.

Barbara was born with a particular temperament and abilities that blossomed in her childhood. As an adult, she made many choices that changed the course of her life and she was also a victim of circumstances beyond her control. Where, then, do we begin if we want to pick apart Barbara's history to figure out how she can feel more fulfilled now?

I've put dozens of baby boomers' lives under the microscope. To assist me in this analysis, I had at my disposal their answers to the same set of questions from their college years through their fifties, as well as enough details about their careers and family lives to sketch out a picture of how their lives evolved. In this book I share with you not only data from my research on this group but also my own ideas about what might have shaped their lives as they grew through adulthood. My hope is to use this factual data, and my clinical experience, to explore the factors that shape people's lives, support or reject the assumptions we make about what will bring us happiness, and to show whether we can—and more important *how* we can—change as adults. I've used the theory of Erik Erikson to guide my analyses, a theory that posits that adults do continue to develop well past the point of physical maturation. But these changes, Erikson believed, don't necessarily happen in a predictable, lockstep fashion. Understanding how change occurs and how we can make change work to our benefit is one of the key themes of this book.

A Turbulent Time

In the film *The Graduate,* Dustin Hoffman's character floated aimlessly in his parents' pool after finishing college, just around the time all of these students began participating in my study. With the Vietnam War looming as a backdrop, university campuses became the main stages upon which drastic cultural changes were getting played out. A restless and rebellious youth movement offered more choices, both good and bad, to its adherents.

There was also a surge of women students: About 12 percent of eighteen- and nineteen-year-old women attended college in 1947, compared with about 35 percent in 1970. Even in light of these new opportunities, the pressures to conform to a traditional life path were strong. To put into context Barbara's choice to marry, consider that in 1966, on average, women married at age 20.5 and men at 22.8.

Sex and Stagnation: Dominant Views of Development

Credited with discovering that the roots of personality lie deep within our unconscious, Freud, the founder of psychodynamic theory, believed that our personalities are essentially formed by the time we are five, the result of our passing through (or not passing through) sexually oriented phases—notably the oral stage, the anal stage, and, most important, the oedipal or phallic stage. After that it was a matter of playing out the results of one's failure or success at passing through each stage. Though Freud was the founder of talk therapy, he didn't think there was much hope of changing the personalities of people older than fifty— they were too rigidly set in their ways.

Erikson was a psychoanalyst trained by Freud's own daughter, Anna. He spent his time on the playground of the therapeutic institute she directed, watching young children play with their toys. After leaving Vienna and setting up his own shop at Harvard University, where he was to develop his own influential theory, Erikson decided that Freud had misrepresented the process of human growth and change. The more he thought about it, the more convinced Erikson became that our development is shaped by forces other than sexual ones. Just as important, Erikson couldn't envision development coming to an abrupt halt in childhood or even in puberty. That notion didn't fit with his own observations of the lives of his patients and the lives of the famous subjects of his biographical studies.

Although Freud's work fascinated me, and in fact triggered my decision to major in psychology, it was Erikson's work that really engaged my imagination. I was inspired by Erikson's optimism about the potential for change throughout life and by the breadth of his vision about the influences on our development, influences that go beyond sexual motives. Because I was pretty convinced myself, at the ripe old age of twenty-five, that personality continued to evolve through life, I was eager to immerse myself in his theory—and to put it to the test.

Erikson's Building Blocks of Personality

Like Freud, Erikson conceived of personality development as a series of stages. But unlike Freud, he took into account the importance of social experiences throughout our lives. Erikson imagined that at each of these "psychosocial" stages people face a conflict between two forces. If they successfully wage the battle, they will acquire a positive psychological quality. If they lose that battle, an unfavorable outcome will occur. Whatever the result, one stage builds on the next.

To give Erikson's theory the consideration it deserves would require a book in itself, but I've done my best to summarize the psychosocial stages here. I've also, somewhat reluctantly, indicated at what age the stages are most likely to emerge. However, early stages can occur at later points and vice versa. Thinking of them as building blocks rather than stages helps keep this point in mind. The blocks can be combined and recombined in infinitely varying ways throughout our lives.

1. Trust vs. Mistrust
(typically emerges between birth and age one)

The first issue we confront in life is the need to establish a basic sense of trust, or confidence that the world is a safe place for us. If our parents are consistent caregivers, providing food, support, and protection, we resolve this issue successfully and believe that we can rely on other people to care for us in times of trouble. We are confident that the world is a benevolent place, and as we go through our day-to-day lives, we are generally in a good mood.

Jane, for example, is the president of a student theater troupe at a prestigious high school. Whether she's speaking about her husband's recent interest in Mayan culture or her students' efforts to learn a difficult play, she's full of wonder and good humor. She sincerely believes her mentoring can help the kids she works with, and always sees the best in them. Throughout her life, her personality has benefited from the solid foundation she has in her sense of trust, a strength that has allowed her to maintain faith in herself and hope for others.

The people you know who are low in the quality of trust have a fundamental sense of cynicism, and instead of looking on the bright side, they expect the worst of people. They try to take advantage of others because they believe that if they don't, others will take advantage of them first.

Bob was such a person. In fact, he was the polar opposite of Jane, starting out in his college days just about as low on trust as you could possibly be. He gradually dug himself out of this hole, but he continued to be plagued by his low trust in other people. It's interesting to me that, with his personality profile, he chose to specialize in family law, a profession that surely put him in situations on a day-to-day basis where he listened to hours and hours of arguments and bitterness. If anything, exposure to such challenging interpersonal situations would only reinforce this personality profile. Now he is full of regret about how he's conducted his life. Such a difficult beginning definitely presents challenges to fulfillment later in life, but as we shall see in this book, problems even in this fundamental area of personality can be overcome.

We will look at people who span the full range on trust, from the Janes to the Bobs. We'll see how trust served as the bedrock of personality and how people high in this quality throughout life managed to buffer themselves from some of the most unimaginably painful life events. We will also see how it's possible for people who have as many regrets as Bob has to reclaim their lives and reach fulfillment.

2. Autonomy vs. Shame and Doubt
(typically emerges in toddlerhood)

Next in the sequence of building blocks is the feeling that you can trust yourself, a feeling that comes with independence. According to Erikson, if you are able to trust your instincts, you can express yourself spontaneously without running the risk of embarrassing yourself or feeling ashamed. During the "terrible twos," children want to do things on their own, and to do so they need to feel free from self-doubt. Toddlers who can choose their food and toys and learn to control their bodily functions are rewarded with a sense of independence and confidence. Adults who have resolved this period of personality development in a positive manner feel that they are in command of their destiny. They are self-confident and don't frequently question whether what they are doing is right. One of my best examples of this quality was Martin, whose strong autonomy streak in college seemed to prepare him for a lifetime of leadership. A Ph.D. in economics, he takes time off from his successful professional career to devote himself to helping address budget issues facing his local community. Instead of sitting back and just criticizing the local politicians, Martin took action. He joined a citizen's group and eventually became its chair, speaking out forcefully so he could effect as much change as possible.

Those who haven't navigated this stage successfully are afraid of doing the wrong thing. That shame and doubt that Erikson talked about makes them so inhibited and fearful of making mistakes that they engage in rigid or even obsessive routines to give themselves a sense of control. I could see that this was the problem that afflicted Claire, who in college scored in the direction of shame and doubt rather than autonomy. The route she chose to pursue in life was one that was safe and low risk, but ultimately unfulfilling. Now in midlife, she's the type of person who outwardly seems to be doing very well, with a successful marriage and family life. But she feels restrained, uncertain of who she is, and regretful of her failure to take risks when she had the chance.

Autonomy continues to remain an issue throughout our lives, particularly in Western culture, where the need to have control is seen as central to happiness. People like Claire, who find it difficult to stand on their own two feet, may feel unfulfilled because they haven't been able to achieve that ideal. What's more, by failing to take risks, we may actually miss out on some golden opportunities to improve our lives. However, we'll see later in the book that even after a lifetime of feeling afraid of taking risks, it's possible to change your attitudes and take that leap of faith that will lead to greater fulfillment.

3. Initiative vs. Guilt
(typically emerges in the preschool years)

The quality of "initiative" is the enjoyment of exercising your mind, directing others, and enjoying flights of fancy. We develop the potential to acquire initiative during the preschool years, when we are most imaginative and begin negotiating playtime with other children. As we get older, our creative impulses are channeled into thoughts and ideas. Being able to express our creativity is a direct follow-up to feeling that we can trust ourselves (and others). Developing the playful side of our nature allows us to maintain a sense of humor and avoid taking ourselves too seriously. It can also make us fun to be around.

It was this quality of initiative that struck me as prominent in the life of Fred, a guy who in his life decisions showed that he wasn't afraid to chase a whim. Although employed as a pharmacist, he ran a blog that he used to comment on some of the idiosyncrasies of the politics in his local area. He seemed to take great pleasure in covering some of the more entertaining features of life in his small town. He went even further than that in expressing his playful side when he decided to put some of his hard-earned savings into an expensive set of antique model cars, a hobby he enjoyed when he was a kid. I wonder how much thought went into that decision, because it seems to me to be somewhat impulsive. Nevertheless, given the humor that was evident in his online musings, I bet he enjoyed the process of restoring the cars.

The opposite of initiative is guilt, perhaps a strange term to use in this context. Erikson was by training a psychoanalyst, and to him this was actually the quality that developed during the oedipal stage, when children are overpowered by emotional attraction to the opposite-sex parent. Erikson thought it was okay for kids to have these feelings as long as they subsided when the preschool years were over. Those who don't develop well through this stage will be plagued by the sense that they could, would, or did violate social taboos against incest.

Now, how do these qualities play out in adult life? According to this view, adults who have succumbed to feelings of guilt and inhibition are the ones who become not only afraid of risk, but emotionally (and sexually) inhibited. One example of such a person in my sample was Alex, who was beset by these feelings. Her inhibition was accompanied by a set of personality qualities in other key areas as well, deficits that signified a lack of self-confidence and an inability to get close to others. Having spent her working life as a software specialist for a major technology company, Alex married late in life and seemed eventually to work herself out of her college doldrums, showing growth not only in initiative but also in these other key areas. What prevented this story from having a happy ending were the regrets that she now expressed about how she'd chosen to live her life. Alex's lack of fulfillment had its roots in her early inability to escape her self-imposed constraints on her freedom of expression. Can she turn this around and achieve fulfillment? We'll see later in the book how people whose lives are bound by these early constraints do not need to suffer from them indefinitely.

4. Industry vs. Inferiority
(typically emerges between ages five and eleven)

Erikson believed that the next crisis stage in life is that of acquiring our society's work ethic, what he called "industry." Accomplishing concrete results through work helps people feel that they are contributing something of value to their communities, the country, and the world. Children who are encouraged by parents and teachers start to believe in their abilities and sincerely enjoy working hard to get results.

This quality of industry was one of the most interesting personality facets that I studied. Although material success doesn't translate into psychological fulfillment, as we will see throughout the book, it is helpful to be able to apply yourself to the fullest in whatever you choose to do. I found a great example of this in Myra. Based on her high industry scores in college—unusually high, considering, as you'll learn later, that the sample as a whole was pretty low—it was clear that she was a very motivated young woman. She went on to have a tremendously successful career as a statistician. In her fifties, she decided to shift her career interest somewhat and, although remaining in her job, returned to her earlier interest in music history. Her research and scholarly articles on the medieval recorder have since made substantial contributions to the field.

The opposite of industry isn't just laziness, although that quality is part of the picture. Erikson used the term "inferiority" to suggest that behind every underachiever is a belief in one's inadequacy. Outwardly, people low in the quality of industry are the ones who do the least amount possible to get by in their jobs. They usually fail to meet deadlines, turn in inferior work, and resist attempts by supervisors to get more out of them. Ironically, they behave this way despite feedback indicating that they really need to shape up or they risk losing their jobs. Their poor work habits and tendency to slack off lead to further problems, such as being fired, which only reinforces their feelings of inadequacy.

Diametrically opposed to Myra was Doris, who spent a lifetime puttering around from one unspectacular job to another, never investing enough energy into any one of them to achieve any measurable results. After years as a lackluster office worker, she quit her job—probably to avoid being fired—to sell cosmetics from her home. Looking at her chronically low scores on the inferiority items, I could see a connection to the failed business attempts. It seemed to me that because she never believed in herself, she would have continued to shoot herself in the foot with such self-defeating behaviors as not following through on appointments with possible customers.

Unfortunately, Doris's low life-satisfaction scores tell me that she now feels about as unfulfilled as anyone in the sample, and it's no surprise. As we'll see later, it's difficult to get yourself out of a hole you've spent a lifetime digging, but it's still possible. Doris, and other people who don't believe in themselves, can learn to take the steps that will allow them to gain confidence in themselves, even in their late midlife years.

5. Identity vs. Diffusion
(typically emerges in adolescence)

Beginning in adolescence, identification with society's work ethic starts to morph into establishing our own sense of who we are and where we are in the world. It was Erikson who coined the now popular term "identity crisis." He used it to describe the intense self-exploration that we begin in adolescence. People who have a strong sense of identity know who they are and what they want out of life. This self-knowledge allows them to propel themselves in a direction that ultimately will give them the feeling that they have made their own unique imprint on the world. We know now that our identities continue to evolve after that point, but certainly the years of adolescence are crucial because they get us started on that process.

I found Beth to be an outstanding example of an identity achiever in college, someone who in the ensuing decades continued not only to grow in her strong sense of self but also to become one of the most fulfilled midlife adults in the study. Her achievements in the world of architecture had brought her international renown. Unlike some of the people in my study whose outward success was not mirrored by inward gratification, Beth was solid through and through. She was also fortunate enough to find the perfect way to channel her energy into a field that she truly loved. The self-expression that this match permitted propelled her through a life of great accomplishment. I would imagine that she not only enjoys what she does, but she also derives pleasure from seeing the results of her life's work directly benefiting others through the structures she has built. As we will see later, having a sense of congruence, or a match between what you do and what you want to do, is a fundamental component of the fulfillment equation.

Roger, on the other hand, seems to have spent his life on an unsuccessful search for a purpose, beginning in college with a diffuse identity that didn't begin to shore up until this last testing when he was in his fifties. An insurance adjuster by training, he also dabbles in watercolor painting. Although some people can pull off this sort of right brain–left brain lifestyle, such was not the case for Roger. Rather than strengthening his sense of identity, these divergent interests have split it apart. Unlike Myra, who went from one successful career to pursue a new interest across divergent areas, Roger simply lacked the clarity of focus that could propel him through life. Roger also spent a good deal of his adult life trailing behind his classmates in several other psycho-social dimensions.

In this book, I'll analyze the problems faced by people like Roger who cannot consolidate their identities, and I'll give suggestions for how they can reach fulfillment. It is quite possible that they may eventually be able to turn the corner, shore up their identities, and approach the re-mainder of their lives with a more positive outlook.

6. Intimacy vs. Isolation
(typically emerges in early adulthood)

Following closely on the heels of identity formation in late adoles-cence is intimacy—the ability to share at the deepest level our innermost feelings, hopes, dreams, and fears. Erikson believed that we are best suited to true intimacy once our identities are fairly firm, so that we won't lose our own internal compasses when drawn into close relation-ships. When we have committed to that which we wish to pursue as in-dividuals, we can commit to a lifelong relationship with another person. Intimacy involves making a commitment, but just as important, it in-volves the ability to allow someone else to get close enough to us to be able to learn and appreciate our innermost qualities, both good and bad.

It's possible to be in a relationship in which both partners have agreed to stay together but not be truly intimate in the Eriksonian sense of the word. As so many people know all too well, you can be in a legally sanctioned union but not fulfill your needs for intimacy. A true blending of the selves is required for intimacy to develop.

People who are unable to reach this depth in a relationship are emotionally if not physically isolated from others. Erikson regarded es-tablishing intimacy as a task typical of early adulthood, but clearly it is an issue that remains with us throughout our lives. Furthermore, once you've been involved in a deeply intimate relationship, the chances are good that even if that relationship ends, you'll seek out another one, be-cause according to Erikson, intimacy is a quality of the individual, not the couple.

The connection between intimacy and self-fulfillment can work both ways. Having a strong sense of identity can give you the grounding that you need to understand and know your own feelings before you share those feelings with others. However, feeling comfortable in a long-term relationship can also give you a jumping-off point for expressing your identity in pursuits that are close to your heart. This seemed to be the situation for Karen, who earns her living as a stockbroker but seems to pour her true passion into the local volunteer work she does on behalf of a national charitable foundation. With the security of having a husband who supports her as a mother, a career woman, and a community volunteer, Karen is able to transcend the boundaries of her own personal or even family concerns.

People whose scores on this dimension showed that they were experiencing isolation tended to have other problems in addition to difficulty achieving closeness with others, which supports Erikson's point that these stages build on one another. Jonathan's particular deficit in this area would take its toll on other aspects of his life, even though he had risen to the top echelons of national and international politics and had alternated between highly prestigious and well-paid consultancy positions and brief periods in private think-tank enterprises.

Looking at his personality profile, anyone would see that Jonathan had many desirable qualities ranging from self-assurance to an unwavering work ethic. But eventually his feelings of inner loneliness, maybe made more poignant by his many successes in a highly demanding field, caused him to question and doubt his life's accomplishments. You'll learn later in the book how someone like Jonathan can be given another chance at feeling his life is worthwhile. In turn, he may then take a fresh look at the need for intimacy in his life.

7. Generativity vs. Stagnation
(typically emerges in middle age)

We now arrive at the psychosocial issues that are most strongly associated with middle and later life. The first of these, "generativity," is defined most simply as the quality of establishing a connection to future generations. The most obvious route to generativity is to become a parent. However, as with intimacy, having a particular role in life doesn't guarantee that the feelings associated with that role will follow. It's far more accurate to regard generativity as a sense of concern for younger generations, not just the children who are in one's own life. One way to express this concern is through a desire to produce something that will help improve the lives of people in the future. Other ways are to serve as a mentor, supervisor, or counselor. The core component of generativity is wanting to share your knowledge and skills with the young. As you will learn in the book, generativity figures heavily into the notion that the most fulfilled people in the study felt confident that they would be remembered after they were gone.

The alternative to generativity is stagnation, a term that captures the inward attention of people selfishly focused on their own needs. As the polar opposite to generativity, stagnation describes the mental state of people who believe that the young are not worth their time or attention. These are the true believers in that old term "generation gap." You don't actually have to be very old to experience stagnation. Much to my amusement, I've heard plenty of people in their mid- to late twenties in graduate school grousing about the poor work habits of the current crop of undergraduates, who are often just two or three years younger than they are.

In early analyses of the data from my study, I sought to categorize people into "generative" and "nongenerative" occupations in order to try to understand the links between careers and personality development. As I found out soon enough, it wasn't going to be that simple. Proving there is some order to the universe, though, I came across the case of Dwayne, a youth group leader who inspires his young charges to perform at their best. The teens he helps are thankful for his guidance, and he, in turn, seems to have maintained his faith in their potential to succeed. Dwayne's feelings of fulfillment are directly pegged to his confidence in the generations who will come after him.

The reason that a one-to-one correspondence between occupation and generativity didn't emerge in my analyses becomes clear when we contrast Dwayne with Debra, one of the most stagnated in the study. Trained as a teacher, she actually did invest a large share of her life in transmitting knowledge to the young. But simply occupying that role didn't provide her with a surefire route to generativity. Instead, Debra lagged in other psychosocial qualities, particularly identity and intimacy. The growth of her sense of generativity seemed stymied by these deficits. If she's going to be able to experience fulfillment and avoid the bitterness that stagnation can bring with it, Debra will need to make her way through to a more solid sense of her own worth. We'll see later whether such reparation is possible.

8. Ego Integrity vs. Despair
(typically emerges in older adults)

Finally, we face the crisis that Erikson called "ego integrity"—literally, feeling that your self or ego is an integrated whole. We achieve a sense of integrity when, looking back on life, we accept both our successes and failures and have a healthy perspective on life, otherwise known as wisdom.

If we, on the other hand, assess our lives as a series of disappointments and regrets, we run the risk of developing a disdain for our own experiences and the world in general. The despair that accompanies the failure to achieve ego integrity is perhaps the most frightening of all the negative outcomes of a psychosocial crisis. Emerging at any point in life, but most poignantly at the end, it leaves the individual with literally no time to rectify past mistakes. The person in despair is left to stare mortality in the face without hope that an unhappy ending can somehow be rewritten. Think of King Lear as he looks upon his life's failures: "A poor, infirm, weak, and despised old man."

It was this dimension that became the linchpin of my study when, trying to capture the essence of fulfillment, I decided to use ego integrity scores as the key defining measure. Of course, with my sample in their middle to late fifties, they were still technically too young to have confronted this issue in a head-on fashion. However, based on Erikson's premise that the psychosocial issues thread throughout our lives, I found this quality to come the closest to what I was hoping I could capture as a measure of fulfillment.

There will fortunately be many examples of people who achieved favorable resolution on this issue and had high ego integrity scores. I'm choosing to talk about Jerome here because, as successful as he eventually became, it wasn't a straight shot from outstanding adjustment in college to midlife fulfillment. You don't have to just score a bunch of plusses from day one to be a satisfied middle-ager. Jerome began his adult life inauspiciously enough, working in both the nonprofit and small business sectors. Although his personality scores were consistently favorable from college on, judging from his somewhat unstable career history, I had to conclude that he just hadn't found his niche. Perhaps he was feeling pressured by his family to toe the line and stay in business. He eventually found what he wanted, which was to trade in his three-piece suit for the outdoor gear of an archeologist. When he was forty-six, he moved to Arkansas to train for his new career in one of the research stations at the excavation site of a Native American village. His strong faith in himself finally paid off, and he experienced true fulfillment. Suddenly he could look back on his tortured career path with pride because it had led him to where he was.

There was not to be such a graceful ending to Paul's story, at least not yet. His personality development had never been very strong, and that was perhaps why he was unable to withstand the stress of fighting in Vietnam and the aftermath. As we'll see in Chapter 8, Paul's frail personality placed him at risk for suffering the harsh consequences of exposure to battle. After returning stateside, Paul took a variety of jobs in computer programming, but never held on to one for very long. By the time of the study, he was living in a rooming house in a small town near Milwaukee. He drifted away from his wife until, by his midfifties, loneliness and despair were his primary feelings. Paul will have great difficulty reversing his fortunes and finding greater meaning in his life. It's not an impossible task, however. As I take you through the lives of the people in my study who have managed to set their development back on course, you'll see that it is never too late to turn your life in a positive and fulfilling direction.

Psychology's Not All: The "Biopsychosocial" Model

How do we navigate our lives across these eight personality challenges? What propels us through from identity to intimacy and then perhaps back to trust? In Erikson's "biopsychosocial" model of adult development, our personalities form and reform as a result of changes in our bodies, our minds, and the historical and cultural influences through which we live.

I suppose it is most obvious to begin to explain this model by looking first at the biological factors that contribute to the ebb and flow of our lives. We inherit certain tendencies that influence the way we look and feel, and, over time, the way we experience the aging process. But I don't want to linger on the biological too long because it's also pretty clear that our behavior affects many, if not all, of the changes our bodies go through as we develop in life. Drinking alcohol, exercising, smoking, eating fruits and vegetables, worrying excessively, and so on are all behavioral patterns that interact with the actual physical characteristics that make up your body's tissues.

So, the biological facts of life are important, but psychology comes into play pretty readily. Similarly, our personalities are not set in stone. Even the most steadfast of us can respond in uncharacteristically unreliable ways if we're provoked. It's the stuff of either hysterically funny or poignantly tragic great stories. Earlier I mentioned *King Lear*. In that play, everything began to unravel when the narcissistic and egocentric leader's supports were pulled out from under him, in part through his own doing when he rejected the one daughter who truly loved him in favor of the two who spoke falsely of their devotion.

This brings into mind the sociocultural component of the biopsychosocial model. Our families—nuclear and otherwise—are our support systems from the very first to the very last breath we take. The family, though the most important part of our social network, is only a piece of the larger context in which we grow and develop. Hillary Clinton claimed that "it takes a village" to raise a child. That principle extends into adulthood, too.

History and culture set the outer parameters for some of the most important experiences that we have. Very often we don't see just how deeply the personal events in our lives evolve out of these broader social forces. We might blame ourselves for mistakes that we've made without recognizing that we didn't have much choice, or just as mistakenly give ourselves credit for accomplishments that reflected social privilege more than individual effort.

When I think about these cultural forces, I like to imagine them in concentric circles, much as was proposed by the late Cornell developmental psychologist Urie Bronfenbrenner. According to Bronfenbrenner, although we are aware of the social forces that impinge on us most closely in the form of our friend and family networks, even these close relationships occur within a certain time and place in history that ultimately can influence how these relationships change over time.

The biopsychosocial forces in our lives often combine in unexpected ways. For instance, your ethnicity, race, religion, and gender all influence how others relate to you and in turn can cause you to relate in particular ways to others. Sometimes we find ourselves behaving in ways that fit with the image that others hold of us. For example, people who appear to be old are, perhaps naturally enough, treated as old, and then, perhaps prematurely, they start to act old. Our development throughout the decades of adulthood is influenced by these cultural beliefs about what is appropriate for people of various ages.

Understanding the intersection of biological, psychological, and social forces as they influence our development can show us why it is so important to look at variations in how each individual's life plays out. I will make the argument that to reduce development to strict age-based categories that emerge in a lockstep fashion keeps us from appreciating the true complexities that influence events throughout our lives. There is also an unfortunate determinism that comes from believing that age "causes" us to go through certain phases.

You can't change your age. But you can manipulate those forces that set your life in a certain direction. And if you like what's happening in your life and you wish you could stop the flow of time to keep you where you are right now, you can gain insight into how to plan your future so that it will continue to bring you fulfillment.

To the Test

I found much to appreciate in Erikson's theory, but I was left with one nagging concern: It wasn't studied well in real life, over time, as people actually developed. Erikson based his theory entirely on his own clinical experience, his observations of life in various cultures, and his analyses of the biographies of famous people such as Martin Luther and Adolf Hitler. Empirical research just was not his primary, or even secondary, concern.

Little did I know that I would have the good fortune of conducting my own empirical test, which would allow me to find out whether Erikson's predictions about the course of human life would hold true. The opportunity to conduct this test would be a stroke of good luck that would send me on my own journey to begin the investigation of a lifetime.

CHAPTER 2

The Forty-Year-Old Experiment

The process of development has fascinated me ever since I was a child. My father's work in the field of medical geriatrics introduced me to the concept at an early age, and by the time I was in college, I was hooked on the idea of studying how people change over the course of their lifetimes. When I got my doctorate degree in developmental psychology, I decided to start my own program of research tailored to my specific interest in adult change and growth. But I couldn't have predicted the particular direction this would take early in my career. I never would have imagined that I would inherit a unique study, one that has become my life's work.

Inside the Study

The study itself was born in 1966, when I was still in high school and totally unaware of its existence. It was launched at a private university in the Northeast where I would end up teaching ten years later. At the university, three hundred fifty students signed up to fill out a psychological survey in exchange for extra credit. As they entered the classroom at the appointed hour, a young and eager doctoral student—we'll call her Ellen—handed them each a set of mimeographed sheets of paper containing sixty questions, plus a mood assessment. The students had no idea that the very same survey would arrive on their doorstep once a decade for the next forty years.

Ten years later, in 1977, I was a young professor preparing to teach a course on adolescent psychology. I was frantically in search of new ideas to present to my students. I had never taken a course specifically on the development of teens, and I knew about the topic only firsthand from my (somewhat) foolishly misspent youth.

I was already very taken with Erikson's personality theory and wanted to weave it into my course. In the nick of time, I spotted a very relevant article in a professional journal. It was a report of Ellen's study from 1966, the one conducted at the very same university where I was teaching. It was on how college students changed in ways defined by Erikson's theory. It seemed to me that students would love hearing about this study, and by the same token, I thought I would enjoy teaching it. Since college students start out as teens, the study would be a good way to look at the changes that occur as kids grow into young adults. The added bonus was that it was done at their very own school.

After digesting the main findings of Ellen's study, I had a moment of inspiration as I dashed off to class. The study had been supervised by a psychology faculty member who was still teaching at the university. What if I could get in touch with those very same students who would now be in their thirties? Follow-up studies, after all, are the gold standard of research in my field. Here was a perfect opportunity. I would just have to find the original questionnaires, contact the participants, and sit back and watch the data come rolling in. It seemed like a simple plan. But I was wrong about that!

This was way before the advent of email, so I had to put in a few calls to reach the professor who had been Ellen's dissertation adviser. I introduced myself and chatted politely for a few minutes but quickly got to the point: Did he have those questionnaires from ten years ago? My heart sank. Unfortunately, he didn't. He did, however, have the unbound copy of Ellen's dissertation. It was a carbon copy, tenuously held together in one of those old-fashioned black cardboard binders. (It now has a hallowed place in my lab, effectively having become our bible.) As grateful as I was to have the dissertation entrusted to me, it did not contain what I really needed—the actual data linking participants with test scores.

For a few days, I racked my brain, desperate to think of how I could find these people. I didn't want to bother Ellen with my request, and plus, I felt a bit presumptuous, contacting her out of the clear blue sky to ask if I could borrow her very own dissertation data that had taken her several years to collect. But I finally mustered the courage to give her a call. To my pleasant surprise, she was happy to hear that someone wanted to continue her work. But also to my surprise, she no longer had the data. And she had no idea what had happened to it. "The joys of longitudinal research," I thought. There was nothing left for me to do but move on, reluctantly, to another project.

A few months later, serendipity was to step in for the first time, but not the last time, in the course of the study. Although only a new assistant professor myself, I was asked to attend a conference in New York City and work at the job placement table. This was rather ironic in a way, considering I myself had just been hired not one year earlier. I took on the job with relish. How cool it was to finally be on the other side of the interview table! While singing the praises of my university to a prospective candidate, I spotted a name on the name tag of a young man interviewing candidates for another school, psychologist Alan Waterman from Rider University. He was someone whose research on Erikson's theory had become very familiar to me, thanks to the course on adolescent psych. Without being too rude, I hoped, I finished up with my interviewee as quickly as I could and made quick tracks over to Waterman's table. It turned out we had a lot of common interests and contacts (academia is an amazingly small world). Casually, I mentioned my failed attempts to track down Ellen's data. Immediately he laughed and said he knew exactly where the data set was located. He promised to make a few phone calls and get back to me the following week. "What?" I thought to myself. "No, it couldn't be that easy! He must have been kidding. Sure, play a joke on a gullible novice."

But it was no joke. Within two months, I had my hands on a moldy box of IBM punch cards that had been sitting unnoticed for a decade or so in someone's basement in Poughkeepsie, New York. A former colleague of Waterman's from graduate school had inherited them—how, I will never know, but I was grateful for my own little six degrees of separation story. I was ready to embark on the next phase in my detective work—finding the people whose scores corresponded to the tiny rectangular punches on those now somewhat warped white and pink paper gems. If only I could find out how those students had turned out, I could unlock the secrets to how our personalities develop in adulthood, and maybe even bolster my hero Erikson's theory. To me, it was an exciting prospect.

Then reality set in. What could I possibly do with these cards? They contained nothing but holes and a string of numbers across the top. And they would continue to mean nothing unless those numbers could be connected to actual people. Emboldened by the luck that had gotten me where I was, I turned next to the college's alumni office, hoping they would help me match names to data cards. I don't know if they wanted to advance science or just needed a juicy story for the alumni magazine, but whatever their motivation, it was enough to let me delve into their treasure trove of names and addresses.

Once I knew which names went with which numbers on the data cards, I composed a letter to the 349 former students, reproduced the original questionnaires, and added a brief form on which they could write down their updated work and family histories. I lugged the box of letters to the post office, sent them off, and hoped for the best.

Soon enough, completed questionnaires began trickling in. I opened each envelope with great anticipation, wondering what adventures had awaited each participant in their postcollege years and, more important, how they had felt about those adventures. How had their college hopes and dreams evolved over time? What excitements and disappointments had life thrown their way? How would these changes prove or disprove Erikson's theory? Plus, I had an ace up my sleeve. I had also given the same questionnaire to students who were now in college, at the same university. How would college students from the antiwar era of the sixties differ from those of the pro-establishment seventies? Were there some universal truths that transcended the two decades?

To think that I would be able to answer all of these questions gave me a preview of the wonderful sense of accomplishment I would eventually feel thirty years later. Those emotions were only reinforced once I analyzed the data and the findings began to emerge. From there, it was relatively easy to get the paper, which I coauthored with Alan Waterman, published in a scientific journal. Our study became the first not only to follow people over the decade or so after graduation, but also to make key generational comparisons. Just as Erikson had predicted, the students developed and changed quite a bit in that first decade of adulthood. My work was now officially done, my points were proven.

And yet . . . a few years later, I grew curious about that group in search of extra credit back in 1966. Penn State psychologist Sherry Willis, a friend of mine who is a preeminent longitudinal researcher in the field of intelligence, casually asked me when I would be publishing the next wave of my data. I had moved on to other areas of investigation, but the more I thought about it, the more I realized that she had made an excellent point. Why not follow up with the students again? By now they were in their early forties. It might be interesting to see whether their personalities had continued to change. The notion of the "midlife crisis" was firmly entrenched in the public's mind, and it seemed like I might be able to provide some data that would tell us whether or not the phenomenon really existed.

Once again, I approached my participants, and once again I was rewarded with freshly updated surveys. Their responses were more complex this time, as their life stories had understandably taken more twists and turns in the ensuing years. As I read through their answers, I felt like I was reconnecting with old friends. I found out whom they had married and unmarried, how their families were growing, and how their earlier career decisions were panning out. I was so glad that my colleague had suggested I do another follow-up study—in fact, I don't know how I ever could have thought of not doing it.

Now that I was hooked for good on the joys of studying lives over time, I was more methodical about how I would complete the fourth round of testing. I accepted a graduate student, Joel Sneed, into my program who said that his number one desire was to help me run the follow-up. (The time for it was drawing near.) However, we soon encountered a stumbling block. With the passage of time, it was getting harder to find some of the participants, and our numbers had dwindled. Unless we came up with some creative solutions, Joel wouldn't have enough respondents around which to build his dissertation.

We decided to use the increasingly popular Google search engine to hunt down some of the "missing" subjects. Sure enough, not only did their names pop up fairly readily, but so did many of their addresses, phone numbers, and email addresses. Occasionally even some rather personal information showed up in our preliminary forays. Intrigued and encouraged, I made it my business to spend the summer of 2002 looking far and wide for my lost participants. Finding them was one thing; getting them to agree to fill out the questionnaires was another matter in some cases, as it took a few tries by way of pleading emails before they finally came through. Having gotten so close, the suspense was really almost too much to take. Now that I "knew" them from my Internet snooping, I was more curious than ever about what their responses to my questions would be.

Persistence paid off, and by 2004 we had surveys from more than half of the original three hundred fifty subjects. It had been forty years since they'd first filled out the surveys for Ellen. And now I could see that indeed their personalities and life paths were not set in stone or marked by predetermined milestones. They were far more fluid than our culture would expect them to be, yet I did discover some distinct and unexpected findings and patterns.

The Six Major Findings

When I started analyzing my data—putting together the pieces of this forty-year-old puzzle—I had some ideas of what to expect. Erikson's theory, for example, tells us that people tend to go through a more or less regular pattern of developmental changes, although even he hedged on this by pointing out that any stage can emerge at any age. I was willing to leave it at that, and given that I was venturing into previously uncharted territory, I kept an open mind as I tracked how the participants had changed since their college days. I hoped I would be able to see how historical and social events had affected their life paths, and compare those external forces to more personal or internal changes for each participant.

I spent five years scrutinizing everything from those ancient punch cards to the outpouring of information that I had gotten from my most recent follow-up. At the end of that intense analysis, I came away most intrigued by the following six findings, either because they fit my expectations or, even better, because they did not.

1. School was not a top priority for this group— but they succeeded anyway.

In analyzing the data from my first follow-up, when I compared college students in the 1960s with those in the 1970s, I was struck by the overwhelming fact that the "industry" scores of the first group were astonishingly lower than those of their younger peers. I thought that people in college, particularly students at an expensive institution with high academic standards, would want to study hard. But the majority of those in my study didn't have a very strong work ethic when they were in college. In fact, those 1960s college students had lower industry scores than any students I have tested since, including the Gen Xers from the late 1980s and the millennium generation of the early 2000s.

If you're a baby boomer who was young in the 1960s, you can probably guess what some of the reasons were behind the participants' low desire to achieve. Here's what I came up with as an explanation. For one thing, drug use was on the rise. Although the college these people attended wasn't at the vanguard of the marijuana movement, the influence was definitely a real and present force. Second, a number of the people at the college were from relatively well-to-do families and their future place in society was not too much in question. Since their families were well connected, they knew that if they didn't do that well in school, they would still probably be given the chance to study medicine or law.

At the same time, the Vietnam War was just beginning to take hold in the consciousness of the young. Students were beginning to protest the war and the establishment values that it represented. Consistent with these protests was the notion that you should put your energies into dismantling the status quo, not toward your schoolwork. Teach-ins replaced classes, and as spring finally warmed up the grassy quadrangle, studying seemed to be a less and less relevant activity.

After college, however, even the rebellious members of my sample began to toe the line. Their sense of industry showed a dramatic upsurge, and they quickly became the hardworking young adults who would turn into successful lawyers, physicians, politicians, and business executives. Their rebellious mind-sets would fade as the 1960s became the 1970s and their twenties became their thirties. The deep dip in industry they showed in college would not characterize them for long.

This finding is a stark example of how we are the products not just of our individual motivations and quirks but of our historical eras. Some scholars argue that our worldviews and values are most influenced by the events of our late adolescence and early adulthood. To a certain extent, my findings reinforce this perspective. However, these findings also go beyond this interpretation and show that, as you will learn shortly, we are not fated to stay within the lines sketched by these early-adult experiences.

Since individual stories are always more interesting than group summaries, allow me to introduce you to an exemplar of low industry among my survey participants, Phyllis. At the end of college, Phyllis still hadn't mapped out her life's direction at all. She headed off to Key West, where she could spend as much time as she wanted to out in the sun. Eventually she drifted into a teaching job, where she earned enough to keep herself financially afloat.

Within a few years, she moved away from her carefree existence to the more conventional role of wife and mother. Phyllis typified many of the people I studied of this generation, whose young adulthoods were unproductive anomalies in otherwise productive lives.

2. Something was missing from life in the 1980s.

After graduating from college, the members of the sample began to get involved in the "establishment" that many of them had once so firmly rejected. As they matured into their midthirties, they were now being swept away by the superficiality of the Reagan-era clichés—big cars, red suits with shoulder pads, the television show *Dynasty*—all reflecting the materialism of the time. Those with money reveled in the tax cuts and the trickle-down economy that allowed them to spend money on themselves.

As I started to analyze my sample's data from the late 1980s follow-up, I found myself again puzzling over what I saw. Scores on Erikson's stage eight—ego integrity—were at a low point. But people younger than my subjects also scored low on ego integrity during the 1980s. They were all infected by the bug of the "me" generation. The Reagan era's focus on the outward trappings of material success was based in large part on the belief that people should save their tax dollars for their own personal use. They rejected with a vengeance the ideals of previous decades that advocated that the more affluent should help contribute to the sustenance of the less fortunate.

Yet again, I was seeing how particular historical eras affect the development of our psyches. The 1980s eroded the lofty goals of the 1960s. I could only hope that things would turn around in the 1990s, if not for everyone in the sample then at least for some. Otherwise, I could envision only a very bleak future for them and for their kids. Erikson said that if children are to develop basic trust, their elders must have a sense of ego integrity.

There was, however, good news. By the most recent testing, several of my participants had indeed made significant turnarounds in this key area of ego integrity. One of the most marked was the transformation of Ira, who made a radical career shift during the 1990s. Scoring his questionnaire, I let out a little cheer when I saw the spike in his ego integrity scores. Back in the eighties, he had successfully progressed up the financial career ladder, but he did not seem to be a happy man at all. Now he had given up his three-piece suits for the tweedy uniform of the professoriate—he was teaching the young about how to reinvent a world that was facing the challenges of global warming, poverty, and disease.

Not everyone showed such a dramatic turnaround, but many did, and on average, baby boomers in my sample were beginning to think of others and were trying to find a larger sense of purpose in their own lives. We'll be reexamining this question in Chapter 11, but for now, suffice it to say that these aging baby boomers have a higher purpose in mind than just feathering their own retirement nests.

3. They became more generative in middle age.

As I mentioned earlier, when the study went on hiatus after the last paper was published in the mid-1990s, I wondered what would happen to the participants during their midlife years. Would they undergo the infamous midlife crisis or would they weather their forties with relative calm? Would they even change at all? After all, the idea that adulthood is a time of personality stability is a popular viewpoint among psychologists who believe we are each characterized by a particular pattern of traits or enduring dispositions.

Especially important to me was the question of whether the group would increase in the quality of generativity. After all, Erikson regarded a person's forties to fifties as the peak time for generativity, or feelings of care and concern for future generations. If my participants were going to change at all, I predicted it would surely be in this aspect of their psychological functioning.

I am not a patient person, but longitudinal research requires waiting a very long time to see whether your predictions will pan out. It was this question of generativity that was burning in my mind when, finally, on one cloudy New England afternoon I sat at my computer ready to find out the answer to my decades-long quest. I pushed the "run" button on my data analysis program and at last got my answer. There it was, a small but discernible blip of an increase on this key personality quality of generativity. And as I delved further into the data, I could see that the small drift upward in scores reflected a variety of trajectories. Some people increased on this quality a tremendous amount. Others didn't change at all, and then there were those who, sadly for them, became less generative as time went on.

Having satisfied my primary inquisitiveness about overall trends, I was then ready to explore the next question: What accounted for the varying patterns? Was it having children that made people more generative? Most of the sample participants were parents, stepparents, or adoptive parents, so there weren't many childless people to compare with the parents in the group. I kept chipping away at this question and ultimately found that it was the people who became parents early in their adult years, before turning thirty-one, who showed the greatest generativity increases. Something made them want to (or able to) have children; once they became parents, the effects reverberated on their personalities, and their caring and concern for the next generation increased even further.

If you're not a parent by your thirties, though, that doesn't mean you can't develop this fundamental personality quality. Brenda, for instance, is an excellent example from my study. She was a physical trainer for almost twenty years, fulfilled with a job that never became boring to her. Even though at times her clients may have seemed unwilling or unable to improve, she still felt that she was having enough of an impact on their lives to make it worth her time and their money.

The lingering doubt that seemed to persist in Brenda's mind about the direction her life had taken was the fact that she did not have children. So at the age of forty-two, she applied to be a foster parent and, soon after, adopted twin girls. Twelve years later, Brenda clearly looks back on that decision as the best one of her life. Brenda's route to achieving generativity was an unusual one, but it illustrates my study's finding that middle age is a time of exploring and redefining the way we foster the development of future generations. Whether through family, creative accomplishments, or volunteer work, the search for generativity is a defining feature of midlife. The main point is that you feel that you are leaving something behind of yourself that will last into the future. It really is "generativity," meaning a transmission across generations, but it can also be leaving behind creative products that people of all ages can enjoy and grow from.

4. If you get off to a late start, you can "catch up."

Brenda's example provides us with some insight into another of my study's major findings, one that I wasn't able to observe clearly until my participants reached their middle to late fifties. This was a finding that applied particularly to the qualities of identity and intimacy, the personality characteristics that Erikson associated with the early adult years. He clearly included the proviso that any stage can be encountered at any age, and my study provided key evidence on that very point.

The patterns of growth that I detected in my data showed that people who were well past the chronological age when they would normally be confronting the issues of "youth" could continue to resolve these developmental crises or issues. By their fifties, if not before, most of the participants had managed to pull out of their ruts. Their personalities blossomed and so did their satisfaction with their accomplishments.

Most people in the study did in fact in their teens and twenties develop a sense of identity and a desire for intimacy. But hope was not lost for the stragglers. Well into their forties and fifties, many of them seemed to be wrestling with the traditionally youthful issue of achieving self-definition.

The story of one participant especially fascinated me, because the outward signs of his life's success were so discrepant from his rocky beginnings. Soon after college, Andrew married and began what was to be a highly productive career in the field of pastoral counseling. But surprisingly, his identity scores were far lower than those of his peers, some of whom had come nowhere near his level of accomplishment. What inner conflicts and insecurities stood in the way of his development through most of his adult years? Like many of the other highly "successful" people in my sample, Andrew's outer persona did not match his inner state. Although active in his profession and striving to appear in charge, he felt that he at times was only acting a role rather than feeling truly connected with his life choices. It would take him most of his adult life to achieve a degree of comfort with who he was and where he had chosen to direct his life's work. How he reached this resolution became one of the driving forces behind my search for pathways through adulthood. Clearly, we don't all travel the same road at the same pace.

5. Individual differences are important in understanding how people change.

It's both easy and comforting to look for generalizations when we try to understand ourselves and the people we know. How much simpler it is to say that "men value independence" and "women value relationships" than to take a more nuanced view of understanding gender and personality, namely, that some men value independence, but so do some women.

Generalizations save us mental effort by letting us latch on to a kernel of truth within an otherwise overwhelmingly complex set of ideas. Why does my friend engage in self-defeating behaviors such as coming in late for work or losing her temper around her boss? Rather than try to unravel all the factors that may lead to her undoing, I try to find a salient reason: Maybe she's menopausal!

Even if they are somewhat true, generalizations get in the way of our being able to understand what makes us tick, particularly when we are trying to examine lives over time. If we conclude that people are a certain way "because" they are a certain age, how can we then account for the fact that some people show more or less of an attribute? For instance, we've already seen that people in the study gained in generativity overall. But that pattern did not hold true for each individual participant. As we examine lives in depth throughout this book, we will try to understand why and how people differ in their personality development. Learning about these differences can help each of us maximize our own well-being and happiness.

What makes the study of lives so compelling is not only differences in patterns of personality and behavior but also the fact that people can start with very similar backgrounds and yet deviate in radical ways as their life directions take different twists and turns. One of the generalizations that people tend to make is that as we get older, we become more similar to other older people, usually not in ways that are considered good, such as becoming "senile" or "dependent." But gerontologists have now established that as we get older, we actually become more different from one another. This is in part because the decisions we make early in life have a cascading effect on the changes that happen later. Each choice has an effect on the subsequent events that happen to us, and with the passing years, these choices cumulate into larger effects.

Let's look at two of the participants in the study who shared some of the same defining experiences when they were young—namely, the pre-law path in college. The university was well-known for this program, which in fact was one of the most competitive in the country. It was natural that prospective lawyers would choose to attend this school in order to increase their chances of fulfilling their dreams. Arthur and Sam were both accepted into this challenging major, but after they got their college degrees, their lives began to diverge. Arthur went straight on to law school, and Sam took a detour of two years, entering a master's program in philosophy. Sam's low identity scores in college seemed to echo his indecisiveness, and so even at this early age, the two participants had begun to pursue their diverging pathways. Still, by their early thirties, both Arthur and Sam were partners in law firms. But psychologically, Sam was heading in a more negative direction than Arthur, as Sam struggled more and more in the area of identity.

After ending a long-term relationship with a woman he met in graduate school, Sam became involved with a male partner with whom he still lives. His pattern of low identity scores, from college through the present, suggested to me that he was struggling with issues faced by gay men of his generation adjusting to social discrimination against homosexual relationships.

By the time the two men were in their fifties, their life patterns had taken significantly different turns. Sam, although apparently in a satisfactory relationship, from an emotional point of view, with a male partner, still felt that he did not "fit in," while Arthur was the proud father of two children who had followed him in his profession and were themselves already very successful. Sam's unhappiness had spilled over from his continued quest for self-definition into feelings of frustration and uncertainty about his life's purpose.

6. The baby boomers are not, as is claimed, selfish narcissists.

We hear a lot of talk in the media to the effect that the baby boomers are a generation interested primarily in themselves and in meeting their own insatiable needs. As they retire, they look to extravagant diversions such as cruising around the world or gilding their already expensive condos. They are supposedly afraid of growing old and, as a result, are willing to spend small fortunes on cosmetics and anti-aging products. That's what advertisers would like us to believe, and certainly those who pitch their products to this age group are convinced that this is true, or they wouldn't be pitching these products so hard.

To be sure, in other research I've conducted on how middle-aged people feel about the aging of their bodies, I have encountered a certain amount of what I would call middle-aged "whining." Compared with their elders, midlife adults are more concerned about wrinkles, problems with their eyesight, and getting fat.

But are beauty and youth the baby boomer's major preoccupations? We'll see in the chapters to follow that yes, to be sure, there are some narcissists in the crowd. (There always are, in any crowd.) But most of my participants are not just out for themselves. They are concerned with their children, the world at large, and social causes that take them outside their own narrow range of concerns, both physical and financial.

Advertisers have missed the mark if they think that they will sell products by appealing only to the vanity of the baby boomers. It is true that many baby boomers are receptive to the advertising messages, but these skin-deep products are not what they are ultimately seeking. They want to feel vital and engaged from the inside, not just be youthful-appearing from the outside. And as the baby boomers get older, their desire to improve their souls and their spirits will only increase.

Many of my participants made life-altering decisions that allowed them to achieve greater self-expression and growth. As I learned about their accomplishments, I marveled at their courageous choices, which sometimes involved leaving behind well-paying jobs, comfortable surroundings, and secure futures to venture off into unknown but more fulfilling territories. These people were seeking ways to expand what must for them have felt like stale and unrewarding lives, and the choices they made played out in continued personality growth in Erikson's key qualities of generativity and ego integrity.

One such person is Vincent, a long-term counselor at a private high school in Texas. Over the years, he took on additional responsibilities not included as part of his original job description, but overall, he spent years on a steady path.

Then a destructive hurricane hit the region, exposing the fault lines of class and race in his town. Amazed at how blind he'd been to these social problems, he decided to grasp the opportunity and do something about them. Although he had known about his school's foundling community service program, he hadn't paid much attention to it, but now Vincent saw that he could use this funding to make a difference both on his campus and in his devastated community. His mentoring program would link the student leaders at his school with at-risk high schoolers. Students appeared from out of the woodwork to apply, and pretty soon community service had become a major focus of the administration. Vincent didn't care about the recognition; he was gratified to have done something with his life that will have lasting impact in his community.

By highlighting these six major findings, I hoped to share with you some of the excitement I have felt in watching my study come to fruition. There are definite messages in these findings, messages that will reappear as we explore the different life pathways that can lead us to fulfillment. The details of my study's method also contain some object lessons about the unexpected routes our lives can take. If someone had told me when I was beginning my career that I would one day be holding on to a set of data from nearly two hundred people that would span nearly forty years, I would never have believed it. Now that my life pathway has taken me in this direction, I am eager to share my story with you.

CHAPTER 3

Which Pathway Are You On?

Before we explore in depth the pathways and the stories that go with the pathways, I will give you a chance to test yourself and diagnose where you fit into the big picture. It's certainly more interesting to learn about someone else's pathway once you know where you stand, and it is definitely more helpful for you to see what pathway you're on before learning how to maximize your own ability to achieve fulfillment.

To arrive at the pathways, I started with the most important information I had at my disposal—scores on the Eriksonian questionnaire that was given to participants from their college days forward. Individual items and scores from the questionnaire scales formed the backbone of my approach and provided me with the empirical basis that is required for valid research. Added to these scale scores were the ratings the participants gave of their feelings of current satisfaction in the areas of work, family, and overall life.

Next, I adapted a method I'd honed in an earlier interview study I'd conducted on midlife adults as a way of understanding how life narratives are formed and modified in relationship to our views of ourselves. In this earlier study, I pieced the interviews together into a coherent story line that gave me a sense of the arc that a person's life had formed and how the person was accomplishing (or not accomplishing) his or her most valued goals. I employed this method of developing a narrative or "life story" in the present study, although I had only questionnaires, not interviews, as the basis for these analyses.

Finally I put on my clinical hat. Using my interpretive skills as a psychologist, I combined all the data into a personality profile, much like the type that a psychologist completes when she performs an assessment. With those personality profiles in hand, I could then start to see if they would form coherent groupings. Before long, the pathways began to emerge, and after some trial and error, I arrived at the final set of five. Later, returning to my empirical training, I went on to validate the measure of the pathways that you'll read about next.

Erikson's stages were the jumping off point for the pathways, but because Erikson's model doesn't give us a consistent picture about how people might differ as they negotiate the stages, the pathways and the stages do not completely overlap. Some of the key concepts I used in generating the pathways did come from Erikson's theory. Particularly important to me were the stages involving identity and ego integrity. Both of these play out in crucial ways in the pathways because they help to define the extent to which a person feels fulfilled and "whole." But I also drew heavily from Erikson's concept of generativity, a central issue that emerges in full force during the midlife years.

Those who never solved their identity crisis ended up on a path without a clear destination. Those who were unable to achieve ego integrity were unable to move on a path that later in life would lead them toward generativity, where they could feel that they were giving of themselves and helping others.

Take the Pathways Test

Now you, the reader, can answer a set of questions that will allow you to diagnose your own pathway. Although scores for Erikson's stages provide important basic data, they don't pertain directly to the pathways and can't give you the information you need to determine which pathway you're on. To make that connection more direct, I reworded the items to capture the distinctive patterns and characteristics of each pathway.

After you take the Pathways Test, you'll have a chance to see how you score. Each question will also be explained so you can understand how it ties into its associated pathway. It might be interesting for you to give the test to someone you know well and ask that person to answer the questions about you (and vice versa). Sometimes others see us more clearly than we see ourselves; at other times, they are unable to judge our true qualities and that in and of itself can provide us with important data.

Try to reflect on both the positive and negative aspects of your personality and circumstances while reading each question below. Be as honest as you can as you answer simply with a "yes" or a "no." Remember, unless you do get someone else involved, no one except you will see the answers that you give. The best way for you to benefit from the test is to tell the truth.

THE QUESTIONS

Seeking Your Pathway

1. Have you met the goals of your youth, when you thought that you could achieve anything you wanted to?

2. Do you feel that you are still searching for direction in life?

3. Is what you're doing now with your life what you thought you'd be doing now?

4. Do you feel that you are running out of time to achieve success in your life?

5. Is it clear to you what your life's purpose is?

6. Have you ever questioned or wondered about whether your life has gone the way you wanted it to?

7. Does making changes in your life cause you to feel anxious or worried?

8. Do you ever take risks in major life decisions just to try something new?

9. Is it important to you that your life is predictable on a day-to-day basis?

10. Do you agree that the old days were better than the present?

11. Are there major decisions you made in life that you now regret?

12. Do you feel that you have been the target of discrimination that has hurt your life's direction?

13. Have you ever felt that you "sold out" on your dreams of youth?

14. Do you think that your life has been harmed by random forces outside your control?

15. Are you ever convinced that your success in life has come too late to do you any good?

16. Have you suffered a major loss involving yourself or your family that you feel you have overcome?

17. Even though life hasn't gone exactly the way you planned it, do you feel satisfied?

18. Do you feel that your early life didn't prepare you well for what was to come in the future?

19. Are there ways that you think you could have adapted better to the rough times in your life?

20. Do you feel that you have strength enough to get you through the future challenges you will face?

21. Did you ever make a major change in your life in order to achieve a greater sense of fulfillment?

22. Do you feel that your ideal self matches who you actually are right now?

23. As you have gotten older, do you think that you have become more like your true self?

24. When you think about your life, do you tend to focus on what has worked out well for you?

25. Are you open to considering options in your life in order to feel more fulfilled?

Score Yourself

1. 1 point if you answered "No," 0 points if you answered "Yes"
2. 1 point if you answered "Yes," 0 points if you answered "No"
3. 1 point if you answered "No," 0 points if you answered "Yes"
4. 1 point if you answered "Yes," 0 points if you answered "No"
5. 1 point if you answered "No," 0 points if you answered "Yes"

Add scores for 1–5 ____

6. 1 point if you answered "No," 0 points if you answered "Yes"
7. 1 point if you answered "Yes," 0 points if you answered "No"
8. 1 point if you answered "No," 0 points if you answered "Yes"
9. 1 point if you answered "Yes," 0 points if you answered "No"
10. 1 point if you answered "Yes," 0 points if you answered "No"

Add scores for 6–10 ____

11. 1 point if you answered "Yes," 0 points if you answered "No"
12. 1 point if you answered "Yes," 0 points if you answered "No"
13. 1 point if you answered "Yes," 0 points if you answered "No"
14. 1 point if you answered "Yes," 0 points if you answered "No"
15. 1 point if you answered "Yes," 0 points if you answered "No"

Add scores for 11–15 ____

16. 1 point if you answered "Yes," 0 points if you answered "No"
17. 1 point if you answered "Yes," 0 points if you answered "No"
18. 1 point if you answered "No," 0 points if you answered "Yes"
19. 1 point if you answered "No," 0 points if you answered "Yes"
20. 1 point if you answered "Yes," 0 points if you answered "No"

Add scores for 16–20 ____

21. 1 point if you answered "Yes," 0 points if you answered "No"
22. 1 point if you answered "Yes," 0 points if you answered "No"
23. 1 point if you answered "Yes," 0 points if you answered "No"
24. 1 point if you answered "Yes," 0 points if you answered "No"
25. 1 point if you answered "Yes," 0 points if you answered "No"

Add scores for 21–25 ____

THE ANSWERS

Finding Your Pathway

If your highest score is for questions 1–5, your pathway is:
Meandering Way

If your highest score is for questions 6–10, your pathway is:
Straight and Narrow Way

If your highest score is for questions 11–15, your pathway is:
Downward Slope

If your highest score is for questions 16–20, your pathway is:
Triumphant Trail

If your highest score is for questions 21–25, your pathway is:
Authentic Road

Note that you may have high scores on more than one pathway, but one set of answers should stand out if you carefully and honestly responded.

The Pathways Explained

Now that you've done the scoring, you'll get a chance to see what your answers mean. Keep in mind that it's the combination of items, not each item one by one, that defines each pathway. You've got to put them all together to give yourself a true diagnosis. Once you've done that, you'll be able to see how each of the pathways played out in the lives of people from my study.

The Meandering Way

The Meandering Way is the path of those who are unable to settle on a clear set of goals and a way to achieve those goals. A low sense of identity is a key feature of this path. Erikson referred to this chronic malaise as "identity diffusion." I've added to the diffusion another piece. I noticed that there were a number of people on this path who seemed to be starting out in life with a tremendous amount of potential—intellectual ability, a solid family background, or other resources. The tragedy for them was that they could not match their accomplishments to their potential. I suspect that they were so competent at so many things, and so convinced of their potential, that they could never get the focus they needed to follow through on one thing. When they realized that they weren't going to achieve their ambitions, they then crashed and burned, despondent that time was running out for good. I wanted to shake those people and say, if you can just come to some sort of resolution, you can start channeling your abilities and do something you can be proud of rather than continuing to fritter away your life. In other cases, I think the antidote to meandering is to take stock, see what you most want out of life, and go after that.

Now let's see what the questions mean

1. **Have you met the goals of your youth, when you thought that you could achieve anything you wanted to?**

   Here we are looking to see if you had that great early potential, the feeling that your horizons were unlimited. You might say no to this because you didn't meet your goals, or because you didn't think you could achieve anything you wanted to, but if you say yes, it suggests you didn't fall victim to the Meandering Way. In that case, though, to avoid some of the traps of other pathways, you still want to keep an open mind to change.

2. **Do you feel that you are still searching for direction in life?**

   If you feel you don't have a life's direction, it suggests you are high on Erikson's quality of identity diffusion, and without a clear identity, you are at risk for the Meandering Way.

3. **Is what you're doing now with your life what you thought you'd be doing now?**

   It's not always a bad thing to be doing something different from what you thought you'd be doing, so saying no to this item doesn't mean you are meandering. However, if your life has veered dramatically from how you thought it would play out, it is a sign that you never actually had a strong identity and that you perhaps need to explore ways to bolster it.

4. Do you feel that you are running out of time to achieve success in your life?

Erikson believed that people who are in a state of despair have a sense that their lives are too short because they won't have enough time left to make up for their mistakes. In the Meandering Way, people believe that they don't have enough time to completely retool themselves and start anew, and they allow this frustration to limit them even more in their ability to become fulfilled.

5. Is it clear to you what your life's purpose is?

You can see why this is an important question for the Meandering Way. If you have no sense of purpose in life, your identity has not been well-formed, and as you reach your later years, your sense of purpose will elude you even further.

There are certainly significant challenges involved in the Meandering Way. Lack of a clear identity, wasting of potential, and fear of life's ending before there is time to catch up make this a pathway that blocks the search for fulfillment. We have an excellent example of a participant whose life fit the Meandering Way in the case of Martha. Here was a woman who clearly had terrific potential when she was in college. Right after graduation she took a job as a human resources manager, an appropriate career for someone with her talents and interests. However, she didn't hold on to that job for long, and instead bounced around from one clerical post to another in low-wage service sector positions. Part of the reason for her thwarted career may have been her decision to marry and raise a family with a man with less education and training than she had. The owner and operator of a small fast-food restaurant, he had her working by his side assisting at the checkout counter.

As time went on, the frustration of not being able to realize the vision she had for her life would take its toll, so that by the age of fifty-five, she felt that her life's dreams had slipped out of her fingers forever. Her low identity scores back in college indicated that she didn't have a very clear image for herself, which is probably why she didn't stay in the field of human services. However, the price she paid for her uncertainty was dear indeed.

If she had been asked what she expected to be doing at the age of fifty-five, it would certainly not have been working the cash register or making sure the french fry machine had enough grease. The large disparity between her ideals and reality led to profound regret, more so than if she'd never had those ideals in the first place. Fortunately for Martha, as my study demonstrates, she can indeed take action and alter what she sees as an immutable course.

The Straight and Narrow Way

The Straight and Narrow Way is a path for those whose lives are characterized by predictability. The people on this pathway shy away from risk and don't enjoy questioning or shaking up their routines. Such stability can be comforting and feel secure, but it also carries a price tag—sometimes quite high—if it keeps their lives so safe that they get stuck. Psychologists talk about the dangers in adolescence to young people who fear questioning their commitments or when they are unable to tear themselves away from the definitions imposed upon them by their families. If you've ever been the parent of a teenager, it may seem like having a child who obeys you would be the best thing in the world. However, from the teenager's point of view, this extreme fear of exploration sets the stage for the development of an identity that, because it is so rigid, can easily break. I often think that the people most at risk for a midlife crisis are the ones who never had a crisis during their youth. They were unable to develop the type of identity that could adapt to life's changing circumstances.

Here is the interpretation of the questions

6. Have you ever questioned or wondered about whether your life has gone the way you wanted it to?

This question taps your identity by inquiring about the extent to which you've engaged in self-exploration. As I've mentioned, Erikson believed that evaluating alternatives was a key to establishing a firm sense of identity in youth. Although the prime period of identity formation is adolescence and early adulthood, it's important to be flexible through-out your life. People on the Straight and Narrow Way don't question the value of their commitments or their accomplishments.

7. Does making changes in your life cause you to feel anxious or worried?

Thinking about change always causes some anxiety, so it's possible to answer "yes" to this question and not be on the Straight and Narrow Way. However, combined with your answers to the other questions, this one provides an indication of whether your desire for stability emerges from fear of the unknown rather than satisfaction with the equi-librium you have now reached in your life.

8. Do you ever take risks in major life decisions just to try something new?

With this question we are looking directly at whether you are able to step outside your comfort zone and do something that requires you to make the conscious choice to change. People on the Straight and Nar-row Way not only feel anxious about change, but they also studiously avoid taking risks, an approach to life that carries with it the cost of re-maining not just stable but stale.

9. Is it important to you that your life is predictable on a day-to-day basis?

Predictability is another important sign that you are on the Straight and Narrow Way. Although no one wants a life that is completely topsy-turvy, the sameness of the lives of people on the Straight and Narrow Way reinforces the anxiety they feel about avoiding major changes.

10. Do you agree that the old days were better than the present?

Feeling nostalgic about the past keeps us from thinking about how we could change in the future. People on the Straight and Narrow Way prefer the old days (or think they do) because they prefer the known to the unknown. We cannot know our future but we can know our past, and this sort of backward time perspective reflects that regressive wish to stick with the known.

Now that you understand the questions for the Straight and Narrow Way, let's take a look at one of the many people in the study who, for better or worse, fit this description. I found those on this pathway by identifying people who had made no major changes in their jobs or families, and then I looked at their life satisfaction and personality scale scores. It was clear that rather than being pleased about this stability, their scores were shockingly low in the scales measuring life satisfaction and ego integrity. After reading their list of successful accomplishments in the major arenas of life, I wasn't prepared for what I found when I scored their questionnaires.

A striking example of the dangers of the Straight and Narrow Way was the case of Albert. Based on his college scores, I think that if you'd asked him at the age of nineteen what he'd be doing when he was fifty-six, he'd have told you exactly what he is in fact doing now. An orthodontist, working in a prestigious practice and living in a well-cushioned suburb of Atlanta, he seems to be fulfilling his youthful aspirations and then some. Back in college, he applied himself more assiduously than most of his classmates, who as we know tended to be slacking off (as reflected in their low industry scores). However, Albert was already heading on the Straight and Narrow Way. Still a hard worker at the age of fifty-five, Albert now seems to face his daily business with a grim determination and without the kind of joy and excitement that true job satisfaction brings with it.

Looking at a person like Albert, who was one of the first people I categorized as being on this pathway, I just can't help but be saddened that he isn't more content with living out the dream he'd hoped to fulfill. Why can't he enjoy experiencing the products of a life of hard work and dedication? Putting it all together, though, I see that Albert's case points out the need to take chances, to experiment, and to continue to be open to change.

The Downward Slope

Next we get to one of the more ominous pathways, the Downward Slope. People who followed this pathway started out with everything going for them, much like those on the Meandering Way. They had tremendous potential and even optimistic views about the future when they entered their twenties. However, something started to go wrong for them very early in life, in many cases as a result of one or two poor decisions. It was hard for them to catch up after that, and like the gambler chasing after a bad bet, they can't get that one success that might help set them in a more upward-leading direction. Others whom I classified as following the Downward Slope are, on the face of things, not in very bad shape at all. In fact, they are highly successful. However, they achieved this success at the price of compromising their core values. Another group that followed the Downward Slope are people who could not rise above forces outside of their control that started to cause their paths to go awry, such as being the victim of discrimination or a fateful accident. We know that many people can overcome even the most horrific challenges. In fact, we will see that with the next pathway. But because these people either lacked the internal resources or didn't have support from others, people on the Downward Slope were unable to handle this adversity. The questions that test the Downward Slope capture these facets of a pathway on which a person's life direction veers alarmingly out of control.

Now you can see what the questions mean

11. **Are there major decisions you made in life that you now regret?**

Although all of us have decisions that we might look back on with regret, serious disappointment with choices you've made can be a sign that your life is on the Downward Slope, especially if you couldn't regroup and recover after those decisions were made. Erikson regarded ego integrity as involving this key feature of being able to accept without regret what you've chosen to do with your life.

12. **Do you feel that you have been the target of discrimination that has hurt your life's direction?**

Being the victim of social discrimination, such as sexism, racism, and, as we get older, ageism, can cause our lives to head in a downward direction that is difficult to alter. People on the Downward Slope not only feel that they have suffered discrimination, but they are also not able to find ways to fight this discrimination in an effective manner.

13. **Have you ever felt that you "sold out" on your dreams of youth?**

Making bad decisions doesn't just mean that you are failing to achieve some form of material success. Some of the people on the Downward Slope pathway had extremely successful lives, but they were lives that conflicted with their core value systems. Their early life decisions are now causing them to feel that they have failed to live up to their early goals, and therefore these people are miserable and bitter.

14. **Do you think that your life has been harmed by random forces outside your control?**

Like discrimination, a random force or accident can cause our lives to head downhill, and such events can also bring with them tremendous personal suffering. Although many people can turn their lives around after experiencing an unimaginable loss (again, as we will see shortly), if you aren't one of those people, you are at risk for the Downward Slope pathway.

15. **Are you ever convinced that your success in life has come too late to do you any good?**

Ironically, people who make decisions in their forties or fifties that significantly improve their lot in life can be unhappier than people who didn't have those opportunities for radical life change. If you have achieved success recently but can't revel in your glory, you may be following the Downward Slope.

The Downward Slope contains several elements, making it one of the more complex of the five pathways. My image of this pathway is that of a descending spiral. One bad decision or experience leads to another, which in turn leads further and further in a negative direction. Even the supposed "success stories" (the late life changer, or the highly paid and well-regarded executive) can fall prey to the dangers inherent in this pathway. More cases will follow in the book, but for now we'll consider Adam, whose life started out well enough when he decided to become an educational researcher, a job that fit with his desire to work toward the benefit of others. After a few years, though, when he realized he wasn't making enough money, he retrained as an accountant. This decision was to have fateful consequences.

By the time the late 1980s arrived, Adam had become increasingly cynical and discouraged by both the political climate and the rise of materialistic values that were taking hold in the United States. He decided to try to turn his feelings around by becoming involved in local environmental causes. He now volunteers his time to help produce a radio talk show oriented toward topics such as global warming and energy alternatives. In some ways, his involvement in this enterprise has served to only reinforce his belief that the country is headed in the wrong direction. With regard to his personal accomplishments, Adam has become resigned to the fact that he will never effect the changes in the world that he once had so passionately desired. Adam's case personifies the "sellout" that I saw in my participants who were successful on the outside but deeply discontented on the inside. In the coming years, Adam will unfortunately be fated to follow the Downward Slope unless he is able to reconnect somehow with his youthful ideals.

The Triumphant Trail

The Triumphant Trail is the path taken by people whose inner resilience has allowed them to overcome significant challenges that could potentially have led them to a life of despondency. In this sense, they are the polar opposites of those on the Downward Slope. I've used the word "triumphant" here to emphasize this element of not just handling or adapting to but actually winning out over adversity. This raises the question: Can you follow this pathway if you've never had adversity to overcome? What if you've had other challenges to overcome that don't qualify as adversity? Sadly, most of us have had some form of adversity strike us. When our ability to overcome it becomes our defining feature, then we fit into this pathway. If we have been blessed by no or only very little adversity, then we can still learn from the diagnostic questions to see what strengths will be needed to prepare us for future challenges we might encounter along the way.

Here is the interpretation of the questions for this pathway

16. **Have you suffered a major loss involving yourself or your family that you feel you have overcome?**

There are two parts to this question—one involves experiencing a major loss and the other involves overcoming that loss. Although you might not have suffered a major loss such as the death of a spouse or child, chances are that someone close to you has experienced a major illness leading to death or disability, or that someone in your circle has suffered a car accident, house fire, or unemployment. Thinking about that event, the next issue is whether you feel you have overcome the loss or event. If you're on the Triumphant Trail, you've managed to achieve some type of resolution and even feel you've grown from the experience.

17. **Even though life hasn't gone exactly the way you planned it, do you feel satisfied?**

We know now that many people in my sample had their lives spin out of control in either a major or a minor fashion, causing them to experience outright failure at worst and disappointment at best. If your life didn't go as planned, are you able to reconcile your mixed feelings about it? If you're on the Triumphant Trail, you have been able to incorporate the reality of your life into a favorable sense of what Erikson talked about in his concept of ego integrity, which is accepting the good and the bad into a coherent whole.

18. **Do you feel that your early life didn't prepare you well for what was to come in the future?**

Resilience, which in Erikson's terms refers to favorable resolution of early personality issues, helps prepare us for the issues that life will invariably bring our way as we get older. He talks about the adaptive ego, or the part of personality that copes with adversity. If you feel that you weren't prepared early in life for what has befallen or will befall you, then you are at risk for not getting onto the Triumphant Trail.

19. **Are there ways that you think you could have adapted better to the rough times in your life?**

This question is in many ways a rewording of the other items that test this pathway. I've included it because, as I said earlier, you may not feel you've had a major loss. I think everyone would agree that life has occasionally handed them some rough times. If you think you could have done a better job of adapting to these rough times, you may be further from the Triumphant Trail than you would prefer to be.

20. **Do you feel that you have strength enough to get you through the future challenges you will face?**

Now, looking ahead, do you feel strong enough internally to overcome the challenges you will encounter in the future? People on the Triumphant Trail have learned that they can handle almost anything, so they will be confident of their ability to work through whatever may come their way in the years ahead. If your abilities to cope have as yet gone untested, then if you have this feeling of inner strength, you will be better prepared to handle life's confrontations.

Finding the people who were truly on the Triumphant Trail, people who had overcome tremendous losses, was an inspiring experience for me. I had a few hints of the tragedies that had befallen some of my participants when I saw their notes to me on their questionnaires about the deaths of children, miscarriages, and the loss of spouses. Expecting to see the worst in their personality scores, I instead encountered some of the most favorably adjusted people in the study, particularly on the key component of ego integrity. Looking back at their earlier scores, I could see the foundation that they had built up in their strong profiles from college, and the mystery was at least partially answered.

I ran into one of the most striking examples of a person on the Triumphant Trail while I was in the middle of coding the raw data from questionnaires, a fairly tedious job but one that I preferred to do myself rather than leave to a research assistant. As I opened the pages of Shelly's form showing her family events, it was a little startling to see the rather cryptic entry on her form that her two children were now deceased. That's it, no explanation, no sense of when their deaths had occurred. My curiosity, as well as my sympathy, piqued, I started to do some background research to discover what had happened. Sure enough, Google revealed some of the details from the trail of news stories reported from her town in Ohio. The unimaginable tragedies had occurred several years ago: One of her children died in college when her apartment was destroyed in a fire; soon after, her nephew, whom she regarded as her son, was killed in a car crash, the victim of a drunk driver. I was certain that the events would have reverberated throughout her personality, cutting a swath across her scores. Amazingly, they did not. In fact, looking further into her current life, it was clear to me that she has had a rewarding career as a pediatric nurse, undaunted by her personal travails. The online evidence of her contributions to charities and volunteer organizations in her hometown portrays a woman who is giving back to her community while her questionnaires at the same time revealed she felt a deep sense of inner peace and contentment. She is truly a model of triumphing over tragedy.

As we learn from people like Shelly, we can gain insights into how we can dig into our own reserves and cope with the harsh circumstances that might come our way. We can't go back and erase past events, but we can try to foster the growth of the parts of our personalities that can lead us to integrate the events into our life views.

The Authentic Road

The Authentic Road is the path of those who continuously examine their life's direction and force themselves to take a bold and honest look at whether it is truly satisfying. To take the Authentic Road, they have to confront candidly the sources of dissatisfaction in their lives and be willing to take the necessary risks to get back on track. Erikson describes the process of identity achievement as one of examining alternatives, and as you've already seen, an unwillingness to engage in this process of reflection can lead to rigidity and fear of change. Now we are looking at the people who continue on in this process of identity exploration throughout their adult years. As a result, they benefit in terms of their enhanced feelings of inner authenticity, feelings that translate into Erikson's stages of generativity and ego integrity in the years of midlife.

Here is the way you can interpret your answers to the questions on the Authentic Road

21. **Did you ever make a major change in your life in order to achieve a greater sense of fulfillment?**

Some people can experience fulfillment in ways that follow from their original life choices, and so even if you're on the Authentic Road, you may not have felt the need to do a complete 180 in your life. If that's true for you, so much the better, as long as you didn't stick to the same set of commitments out of fear of change. Making a change also doesn't necessarily lead to greater fulfillment (as we've seen with the

Meandering Way). However, combining the answer to this question with others regarding the Authentic Road, you get a picture of whether the choices you've made are bringing you closer to your true self.

22. Do you feel that your ideal self matches who you actually are right now?

Psychologists from the humanistic school of psychology, such as Abraham Maslow and Carl Rogers, postulated that we reduce our angst to the extent that we are able to fulfill our ideal selves, what they called "self-actualization." I've added this component to Erikson's stages to capture what I believe to be a crucial feature of fulfillment in midlife. We can always be striving for more, but if we feel that there is a huge disconnect between ideals and reality, the chances are that we will hamper our ability to be fulfilled.

23. As you have gotten older, do you think that you have become more like your true self?

Often, as people get older, they say that they are able to shed their superficialities and get to who they "really" are. In this question, I am trying to capture this developmental aspect of fulfillment. The people on the Authentic Road continue to show increases in their identities even as they make changes in their lives that allow them to express their innermost abilities, interests, and desires.

24. When you think about your life, do you tend to focus on what has worked out well for you?

Many of us engage in a little harmless self-delusion about ourselves, and this positive bias is something that psychologists have identified as part of the healthy personality. It's actually a good thing to focus on your successes rather than to dwell on failures. For people on the Authentic Road, this mind-set is not very difficult to adopt because they actually do think their lives have worked out well for them. If you find yourself focusing on your shortcomings, you can either change what you're doing to allow for greater congruence between who you are and who you want to be or you can take a sunnier view of what you have done and what you think you will be able to achieve.

25. Are you open to considering options in your life in order to feel more fulfilled?

If you're open to change, then you will be more likely to engage in the kind of identity exploration that Erikson regarded as so crucial to establishing a firm sense of self. Considering options doesn't necessarily mean you drop everything and leave your adult life behind, but if you're willing to dream about options, chances are that you'll know when and how to make the move when your commitments are no longer working for you.

As I sorted through the data from the lives of my participants, I was taken on the emotional roller-coaster ride of rooting for those who succeeded psychologically and being disheartened by those whose scores became or remained low. Perhaps most enthralling for me was to see the favorable outcome of a gutsy move by someone who had been unhappy prior to the previous testing but who now had blossomed. You might say that I was living a little vicariously through them, perhaps, but in any case, I never ceased to be amazed by what they were able to accomplish. Such was the case for William, whose story, I must admit, is one of my favorites. He made a transformation in his middle years that was one of the most radical of my participants. He'd begun his adult life by working for a public relations firm, and although things were certainly going well for him there, his personality scores at the time were not those of a particularly happy man. So when I saw that in his late forties he had switched gears in his life, I felt glad he had made these changes. William was now heading up a project in which technology companies come into inner-city schools and provide hands-on training to the students. After applying successfully for funding, William became the institute's first director. Now at the age of fifty-six, he feels that he is fulfilling his mission in life. It was a risky thing to do, but it has paid off in that he is making a difference and helping future generations. Having taken the Authentic Road, his generativity scores shot up, and so did his feelings of satisfaction.

Exploring Your Pathway

The five pathways that emerged from my study of the lives and personality scores of my participants capture the highs and lows of the variety of ways in which we navigate through the many challenges and complexities of adulthood. Each pathway takes part of its definition from different aspects of Erikson's stages, mixed in with key features of other perspectives, notably those that focus on self-actualization.

As you diagnosed your own pathway, perhaps you wished you could be more "triumphant" and "authentic" and less "meandering" or "downward." Maybe you don't think that being stable on the "straight and narrow" pathway is all that it's cracked up to be. What can you do about it? Are you doomed to a pathway that is leading you further and further away from fulfillment? Don't worry. The whole point of my study was to find out how people change throughout life, no matter what track they are on. You've already learned some key lessons about how you can change, starting with the crucial first step of diagnosing your pathway and seeing how to interpret the answers to the questions that define each one. Keep reading and you will learn how to work yourself out of your pathway and onto one that is more fulfilling. My respondents proved over and over that change is both possible and rewarding.

And if you identify yourself as on one of the more appealing pathways, you can learn even more about how to keep enhancing your inner feelings of satisfaction. As you've already seen, being open to change and allowing yourself to consider alternatives is always an important feature of the fulfilled life. The participants who had the greatest inner happiness were willing to examine their options, even when things were going well for them. If we get too set in one groove, eventually even the most triumphant of us can fall into the straight and narrow rut. More important, because we cannot see into the future, we will never know what challenges await us until they are upon us. Learning about how to maintain an open, flexible, and adaptive approach to life will allow you to take those challenges in stride and in the process find how to express your true self.

CHAPTER 4

The Pathways

Many of us have a model of the ideal life in our minds, a model communicated to us since we were little children. The pattern goes like this: You are born, you go to school, you graduate, and you get a job. You get married, have some kids. You keep working, and the kids grow up and move out. Retirement comes. You become a grandparent. Then you prepare to die.

Time for a New Model

This pattern of predictable life changes was fairly common in the twentieth-century United States. The baby boomers' parents, who had their kids in the postwar years, lived by a fairly rigid set of social rules that governed their major decisions. Psychologists and sociologists even had a term for these patterned events: the "social clock." If you were late to get married or early to finish school, you were "off-time"; if you fit the predetermined plan, you were "on-time." Even worse, if you didn't follow the pattern at all—say by remaining single or by not having children—your choices were called "nonevents." Not surprising, those out of step were violating expectations, and thus felt, or were perhaps made to feel, guilty and miserable.

However much it was broken before, by the time the baby boomers came of age, they certainly challenged the social clock. They changed perceptions of what was considered an okay choice and what was considered a deviant one. If anything, conformity was the new deviant in their view. That's why in analyzing their lives I needed to identify a variety of the patterns they followed—and thus I came up with the five pathways. Though each participant's story is unique, there was enough overlap in the participants' patterns to justify grouping them into these five camps. I hope they make it easier for you to think about your life's journey, and to think about how you can change directions, should you wish to.

Although the people in my sample were from the baby boom generation, I believe there is reason to claim some generality for these pathways and not to link them with a specific time and place in history. Thinking back on studies I have done and read about of young people struggling with identity issues, I realize that the pathways in adulthood play out patterns that emerge when people first begin to think about who they are and what they want to do with their lives. It is part of our destiny as human beings to face these issues of self-definition, and we all face the choices that ultimately lead either to frustration and stagnation or to continued growth and fulfillment.

Origin of the Pathways

I came up with the idea of pathways back in the early days of the study, while preparing to give a paper at a conference where I was going to discuss personality changes in the baby boomers. For the session, I used the whimsical title "The Baby Boomers Grow Up." It was one of the first public presentations addressing the maturing personalities of this generation. To tell you the truth, I never really liked the term "baby boomers"—especially in its shortened version, "boomers." But I thought it would be an eye-catching title, and in fact, it was one of the more well-attended sessions of the conference.

Even though I was quite interested in the topic of my lecture, I had some discomfort about coming up with overall trends that are supposed to describe an entire generation of people. It seems so simple-minded to decide that because people share the same birth year, decade, or even generation that they should have identical or even similar characteristics. Yes, all the baby boomers grew up with phenomena such as *The Mickey Mouse Club,* hula hoops, and the Beatles, but even with regard to these icons, the members of this generation differ in how much they cared about them, in how old they were when the phenomena were in vogue (there's a sixteen-year range in the official baby boom designation), and in whether these images were important to their own gender, race, and ethnicity.

There were larger issues that divided this generation as well—some people, like those in my sample, were afforded a college education. Others went as far as high school and never became part of the hippies, the yippies, and the other college-student-led groups of sixties dissidents. While the college students were protesting the establishment's value systems, their working-class counterparts were taking on the adult responsibilities of earning a living, raising families, and, in many cases, going off to Southeast Asia to fight the war that many of the college students were fighting against here at home.

In addition to these larger socioeconomic and sociocultural factors were the individual personality differences that made each individual in the generation unique. The biopsychosocial perspective that gives us this multidimensional view tells us that we have to look inside and outside the person to understand what happens as a person grows and changes throughout life. My particular focus in this study was on personality and how differences among people in psychosocial dimensions such as identity, generativity, and ego integrity interact with people's experiences in the domains of work and family, key areas of adult life. No two people share these constellations of life influences. My job was to try to find the regularities as well as the differences in how people traverse the life span.

So, as I prepared for that talk on the baby boomers, I decided that I would try to capture this notion of individual variation in personality development. My grad students and I have often sat around pondering the question of why some people "go up," some "go down," and some "remain the same" on Erikson's personality attributes. After playing with several possible sources of variation, my statistical analyses told me that the most important influences included level of occupational prestige, gender, and age at first marriage.

However, for this book, which takes a more global approach to capturing the essence of the lives of my participants, I gave myself greater freedom to use a more clinical view. I drew on the entire gestalt of the various forms of information I had at my disposal about each person to look for overall patterns.

My first effort to sort the participants was to categorize them as "stable" or "unstable" in the areas of work and family life. That wasn't a bad way to slice the data, and in fact, the element of life stability still plays into the pathways.

It became apparent, however, that I'd need more than just two groups to categorize the people in my sample accurately. As I read the individual stories of my participants, I began to draft notes about ways that they differed in their life decisions and directions, and I compared these patterns to their personality scores.

Since "stable or unstable" wasn't enough, I also had to look at the nature of the life changes, other circumstances in the participants' lives that might have affected them, and their characteristics when they were younger, before any of these changes took place. Eventually I arrived at the notion of the pathway, and the five different varieties fell into place.

The Many Forces in Play Along Each Pathway

The only truly universals of development are birth and death. As I've noted already, a whole range of biological, psychological, and social factors influence our lives in complex ways, making it extremely unlikely that any two of us will have identical sequences of life changes. Our bodies change at different rates. Our personalities lead us to develop unique ways of thinking and responding to the world. And we are all products of our social classes and our cultures.

In the biopsychosocial model that I've used to understand the lives of my study participants, I've applied a notion that psychologists have found helpful in imposing some regularity on the many sociocultural influences that impact our lives. One set of these influences are the social forces that affect everyone in a given culture, society, or country during a given time period. These are called "normative historical influences." These events include wars, economic depressions, and cultural revolutions. Around the time of my study, there were a number of these— September 11, 2001; the 2004 tsunami; Hurricane Katrina in 2005; and the outbreak of the Afghanistan war in 2001 and the Iraq War in 2003. Like other Americans' lives, the lives of my participants were touched by these historical happenings.

Many of my participants were directly affected by the events of the early 2000s—they were living in New York City with livelihoods that were dependent on the workings of the financial world, the professions affected perhaps most directly by the attack on the World Trade Center. Also included in the sample are diplomats, politicians, and members of political think tanks, many of whom are important figures on the global stage of international relations. Participants who lived in Mississippi relocated after Hurricane Katrina, including one couple who was to live thousands of miles apart after the professional offices of one had to close down in the wake of the large-scale devastation.

Aside from this recent sweep of events, the entire sample of my study lived through the Vietnam War during their college days. Going back even further into their childhoods, they endured the cold war, "duck and run" air raids, rock and roll, and a variety of formative experiences that helped shape the psyches of their generation. The prevailing historical winds caused them to turn away from the middle-class work ethic, at least while they were in college. That is perhaps one reason why they scored poorly on Erikson's quality of industry.

Our life pathways take a particular set of twists and turns as a result of decisions we make, those that are inflicted upon us and those that just seem to jump into our laps. As you diagnosed your pathway in the last chapter, perhaps some of those unpredictable or even uncontrollable forces that have shaped your life came into your mind. Winning the lottery or losing a house in a hurricane are events that influence how we turn out, through not much fault of our own.

Stanford psychologist Albert Bandura once wrote a fascinating article about random forces in our lives, in which he outlined how one event snowballs to affect another. Consider, for example, the impact of your missing a bus that could have led to a job interview that could have led you to a new career path. Perhaps by missing out on the job interview, you saved your life without knowing it, because had you gotten the job in another city, you would have gotten into a serious accident while traveling to a conference or business meeting.

If you think too much about all of these random factors that play into everything you do, you could lose your mind. But there they are, waiting in the wings to shift us this way or that way. And as we go through life, these random circumstances have cumulative effects. They also influence other people in equally significant ways—if you hadn't met the parent of your child, for example, your child would not exist. The point of all of this philosophical talk is to open your eyes to the many ways that your life can deviate from a standard set of predetermined events dictated by the calendar alone.

Don't forget that you can still be the captain of your ship, even as random events may conspire to steer you off course. You can turn the ship around if you are on a pathway you'd rather not stay on. You may remember the 1993 movie *Groundhog Day,* in which Phil, the main character, played by Bill Murray, takes this strategy to a rather fanciful extreme as he relives the same day over and over, with just one slight change each time, until he reaches the outcome he desires. Real life doesn't come with "redos," but we can stop a bad course of events before it reaches the point of disaster or before we are blocked from reaching our most cherished goals. It's not even necessary to make radical changes, because as we've just seen, even one small alteration can have cumulative effects. It's like the sci-fi notion that if an asteroid were headed toward Earth, prodding it into even a slight change of course using a rocket or satellite would be enough to cause it to escape our planet's gravitational pull.

Switching Pathways

So we're not stuck in the pathways we start on. Even though undesired or even random events can make the process that much more complex, with self-scrutiny, and maybe some shaking up from the people around us, we can jump off a pathway and get onto another that will lead to our true mission in life. The goal, after all, is not only to reach fulfillment as an end-state, but also to derive meaning and happiness from the quest itself.

Carol, one of my participants who did make just such a switch, was well along the Straight and Narrow Way in her forties. She wasn't the unhappiest person in the sample, but she was certainly not the most fulfilled at that time, leading a static life in terms of her psychosocial scales, which had remained stable since her twenties. A full-time homemaker raising three children, she had trained to be a social worker but had soon left that behind with the birth of her first child. It was not until her children were in their teens and early twenties that she started to explore reentering her profession. By then, it was a very different world, with new requirements for licensure. After a couple of semesters at the local college, she found that she no longer had a taste for it.

Fortunately, Carol approached her job search as a trial-and-error process this time around, instead of following the path of least resistance as she always had in the past. She eventually found happiness in a part-time job that she picked up at a local photography studio. Along the way, she also became separated from her husband, which certainly altered her historically steady path.

Carol's current life reflects her decisions to find greater fulfillment by experimenting with and ultimately settling on a new self-definition. As a result, she left the Straight and Narrow Way and finally entered the Authentic Road. Now that she's on that pathway, she has greatly improved her fulfillment chances of continuing to find happiness in her future life choices.

A Pathway-by-Pathway Breakdown

I identified the pathways by looking at both the life experiences of my participants and the scores they had received along the way over the course of the various testings. As such, the pathway designations were based on a combination of my clinical judgment regarding what was "really" going on with the participants, below the surface, and what the participants said about themselves on the questionnaires. For many I was also able to compare what they told me about themselves with what the public record was of their accomplishments, both in their careers and in their personal lives. The research method I used would come closest to what psychologists call the "case study." I tried to frame a story about each of the participants and then see how closely the stories fit my pathway descriptions.

In the process of coding each participant into one of the pathways, I noticed that some people who on the basis of their life experiences seemed to be consistent with the characteristics of the Authentic Road did have some significant regrets. Life wasn't necessarily a walk in the park for them. It's also possible that despite these individuals' overall feelings of fulfillment, something tugs at them about what they might have done differently with their lives. My bet is that if this is true, they soon will change, based on their past patterns of changing when doing so was necessary to their overall feelings of fulfillment.

I wanted to get an idea of how many people were on each of the pathways. I already figured that the Triumphant Trail would contain the fewest people, because it was defined by the experience of overcoming extreme challenges. Luckily, at this point in their lives, the majority of participants hadn't encountered significant loss. Of the 182 people in the study, only 10 participants clearly fit this description.

Almost half of the sample (eighty-six people) was on the Authentic Road. Some had arrived there by making changes in their lives in order to achieve greater self-expression. These were the CPAs who became teachers (and in some cases vice versa), the homemakers who sought a professional career, and the lawyers who chose to devote themselves to humanitarian work, to name a few examples. A large chunk of them were people who didn't show significant changes in their life patterns but who seemed to be thriving in their work and family lives. Most likely, they were tinkering around with smaller changes in their lives not particularly visible to the researcher's eye. My sense of these people is that they benefited from the good fortune of having had an open and flexible growth-oriented attitude from their twenties through their fifties, never settling into a groove but always hovering somewhat above that groove, ready to change if need be.

The next-largest group—fifty people—were on the Straight and Narrow Way, located deep within the grooves formed by their decisions to remain static in their jobs, their families, or both. If I'd had to bet on what the numbers would be before I started this process, I would have thought that the Authentic Road and Straight and Narrow Way would have had a similar number of participants, if only because in adolescence we tend to see a fairly even distribution between kids who get into a lockstep pattern based on what their parents think is good for them and kids who like to experiment. However, it made sense that the Authentic Road would by midlife win out, because by that point in life, many people are able to take a step back, for a variety of reasons, and question their earlier commitments. The Straight and Narrow Way can morph into the Authentic Road over the thirty or so years between early adulthood and late midlife.

About 10 percent of the sample fell onto the Meandering Way, characterized by people who chronically vacillate, and the remaining

10 percent were those on the Downward Slope, the pathway for those who make choices that thwart their self-fulfillment.

I predicted these lower numbers based on what we know from the study of abnormal psychology. People in the two most negative pathways are chronically unhappy with their lives, and these numbers correspond roughly to what epidemiologists tell us is the prevalence of psychological disorders such as depression and anxiety. Over the course of their lifetimes, about 18 percent of Americans are estimated to experience depression. A similar percentage will suffer from an anxiety disorder at some time in life. The numbers for these two pathways were lower than these figures, but I wasn't performing official diagnoses. The pathways don't completely map directly onto psychiatric symptoms. My analyses are based on the ebbs and flows of people's lives, which are related to developmental processes that don't fit neatly into the check-box system that diagnosticians use when labeling the ways that people feel and behave. However, it still is useful to know that most people experience moderately favorable lives as attested to by these analyses.

So, overall, your odds are good for getting onto the Authentic Road, but it's by no means a sure thing. I'll be showing you ways to maximize your chance for successfully maneuvering through life so that you can get on that road and stay there. In the meantime, though, I have a few other statistical findings about the pathways that I'd like to share with you.

My search for the pathways began as a way to make order out of what seemed like an almost infinite set of life patterns. This combined with my desire to understand why people changed as they did in the Eriksonian dimensions of the study. I used all the information I had at my disposal to categorize the pathways, including of course the questionnaires themselves. After I finished the pathway coding, I thought it would be interesting to see how the pathways differed both in college and in midlife in relation to the psychosocial dimensions.

One little quirk about this analysis was that the original questionnaire from college actually did not have the generativity and ego integrity scales contained in it, so I couldn't go back and see what the participants were like in these dimensions as undergraduates. But there was still plenty to work with. At a level considered acceptably significant (probability of less than .05, the gold standard in statistics), back when the participants were in college, you could have seen the origins of the pathways they would eventually follow. Those on the Triumphant Trail had the highest trust scores. When we look at that pathway in Chapter 8, you'll see that the quality of "resilience," very closely related to the notion of trust, is fundamental to this pathway. They were also hard workers as students. Their industry scores were the highest of all the groups.

Speaking of industry, a lack of it was the key defining feature of the people on the Meandering Way. Although I tend to think of this group as people with identity problems, I hadn't quite realized just how low their sense of industry would also turn out to be. It took the wisdom of my statistical software program to discern that particular result. The Meanderers had low identity scores—as would be expected—but they also suffered in college from a failure to apply themselves to their work. Their fate would not be sealed by this low score, but low industry certainly made it a challenge for them to arrive at a clear set of goals because they lacked the emotional energy to follow through even on a loosely defined set of interests.

Strong college identity scores distinguished those on the Authentic Road. But almost everyone else, besides those on the Meandering Way, fell into a moderately high range. Where the people on the Authentic Road pathway really stood out was, also to my surprise, the area of intimacy.

When I saw high intimacy scores among those who would ultimately move toward self-fulfillment, I had to give this finding some thought. Following not far behind them in intimacy were the people on the Straight and Narrow Way, and then back many paces were those on the other pathways. People on the Meandering Way and Downward Slope had the lowest intimacy scores of all.

The most reasonable interpretation I can offer is that having qualities that contribute to intimacy also ties into developing a healthy identity and, later in life, working toward self-fulfillment. It's the people who aren't afraid of commitment, who can relate candidly and openly to others, and who can show sympathetic concern—all qualities that define intimacy—who will be most receptive to the type of soul-searching required to get onto the Authentic Road. Their openness with others translates into an open attitude toward their own values, motives, and priorities.

When it came to the personality differences among the people in their late fifties, there was a slight bit of circular logic involved. I relied heavily on those late midlife scores, particularly the identity and ego integrity scales, to form the pathway classifications in the first place. However, as I mentioned, there wasn't a complete one-to-one correspondence between a pathway score and a personality test score. Some people on the Authentic Road didn't have the maximum score or even close to the maximum on the dimension I relied on most heavily, ego integrity.

As it turned out, after I completed this test, the people on the Authentic Road emerged as having the highest scores across the board, just as I would have imagined. However, there were some headline findings in there that I had not predicted. Autonomy and initiative, dimensions that hadn't distinguished any of the pathways in college, were strongest among people on the Authentic Road.

The lowest levels of initiative and autonomy were shown by people on the Meandering Way and the Downward Slope. They would go on to become ever more inhibited and unsure of themselves with each passing year.

However gloomy the situation seemed to be for people whose situations were rather dire back in college, it's still possible to find some hope in the data from their midlife scores. People in all of the pathways ended up doing quite well in the quality of industry by the time they hit their late fifties. Even those on the more negatively heading pathways seemed to be oriented toward working hard and being productive, certainly much more than they had been in their carefree college days. They were ever more invested in learning, using their time well, and performing diligently. It's a finding that parallels results reported by other adult development researchers, who have documented growth through midlife and beyond in some of the qualities that make up conscientiousness, such as deliberateness and a desire to feel and be competent at work.

There were other areas of growth as well. The prospects for people on the Meandering Way and the Downward Slope in the area of intimacy were good—not great, but good. And even though people on the Meandering Way continued to have the lowest identity scores of anyone in the sample, they showed an ever so slight increase between college and midlife.

Several areas of personality growth remained challenges and even became more difficult over time. People on the Straight and Narrow Way, never very strong in the areas of autonomy and initiative, headed downward even further in midlife. As you'll see in Chapter 6, it's very difficult for such people to break out of their habitual ways as they become more and more fearful of disrupting the status quo, even if it's not all that rewarding.

In the next five chapters, you'll read about how a variety of challenges continued to play out in the lives of people on each of the pathways. Still, even as we look at those individuals, I want you to keep in mind throughout the book that no one pathway completely describes every person. I've been successful in imposing some order on what might otherwise be a set of 182 separate lines showing growth, decline, and stability. The truth is that even within the pathways there are vacillations and fluctuations—idiosyncratic trends that reflect the unique combination of the biopsychosocial forces that have an impact on our lives. I encourage you to see where you fit in these pathways, but don't get stuck thinking about whether you will, by necessity or desire, remain locked into that pathway. As you'll see, "Action Plans" for the pathways will help you in that process.

CHAPTER 5

The Meandering Way

Most of us have great potential in our early lives. Some of us have extraordinary potential. But ten, twenty, thirty years later, we may look back and wonder what happened to our shining prospects. Through my study, I encountered many of these types. Had you known these stars on the rise just after they'd graduated from college, you would have been impressed, or possibly even intimidated. Among them were the confident ones, with graduate school acceptances in hand, entrepreneurial ambitions, or prestigious job offers. After college, they went on to earn an advanced degree, start a successful business, or achieve a prominent position in public service. But then something went awry. For some people, that "something" was that they never arrived at an identity. The people on the Meandering Way couldn't make the commitment to a deliberate pathway in life, one that would ultimately pave the way to fulfillment.

It's okay to pursue new directions now and then, but real fulfillment requires that we hunker down and follow through on a set of decisions at least long enough to make sure we like or don't like the outcome. If we continually wander around in search of who we are, we may never have the chance to enjoy the feelings of accomplishment from having succeeded at one thing, even if it was not the perfect outlet for our talents and energies.

Edward

Edward's life exemplifies the Meandering Way, with its multiple twists and turns, all leading nowhere. Out of all the participants' stories on this pathway, it was Edward's that probably frustrated and fascinated me the most. As I saw his life unfold, I could hardly believe what I was reading. It all made sense, however, once I began to look at him as a classic Meanderer.

As I mentioned earlier, I did my own data coding for the study, a task that was at times awfully tedious. But in hindsight, it was the best way for me to think about and analyze the life events of my sample participants. One hot August afternoon, when I opened Edward's questionnaires, I was in for a surprise. In fact, I had to take a step back and make sure I had everything right. Although most people's career history took perhaps two or three lines in the spreadsheet file I was using to enter the data, Edward's took about thirteen. Here was someone who went from one career, in which he seemed on the verge of enjoying a fair degree of prominence, to another that was completely different, where again he seemed to be close to doing well. Each career move seemed almost completely unrelated to the previous one, so that by now he had blown through four or five seemingly promising starts that ultimately led nowhere. What was going on with him?

Intrigued, I thought I would set to work using my online detective skills, and in the process, I found out that since filling out the questionnaires, his life had taken yet another set of turns. In those two years, Edward had moved once again and had started down yet another career path. Living in a small Connecticut town on the fringes of a metropolitan area, he now assisted local farmers in promoting their sales to nearby supermarkets. At times, he appeared on various message boards devoted to the concerns of sustainable farming. Certainly, this was interesting and perhaps even important work, but it had the air of being just one more in a series of inexplicable ventures. I tried to imagine how his life had gotten to this unexpected point. As I put together his personality questionnaires and this new information about what he was currently doing, an image came into my mind of someone who still, in his late fifties, was desperately trying to make an impact on the world but was thwarted by his inability to move forward in any one direction long enough for that impact to be felt. I wondered how he reconciled his rather mercurial past with what I hypothesized was his desire to feel pride in his accomplishments. Did he analyze his previous career stops and starts as signs of a weak identity or did he come up with the rationalization, as many of us do, that his past decisions were the result of other factors? Judging by his low life-satisfaction scores, though, I could see that the rationalization wasn't working very well, if at all.

Over the next few months, I thought often about how Edward had gotten from point A to point B to point C through to point N in what to me seemed like a haphazard life. Summer turned to an icy winter, and as I stared out my office window, I envisioned him alone at his own computer, working away on this most recent business venture, perhaps sitting among a pile of open books, notes, unpaid bills, and empty pizza delivery boxes, pondering the many projects lying in front of him. His email might be overflowing with random questions from his online followers. But judging from what he said in his questionnaires, it didn't seem that he had many real relationships outside his virtual world. He'd cohabited with someone along the way, but that was about it. At the moment, there wasn't much that put joy into his life.

Thinking back on his early years, I could easily imagine what Edward's undergraduate years had been like; many people from my hometown had attended his school and were part of the cohort that preceded mine by a few years. They'd been Edward's classmates. The university attracted high-achievers, and he had likely been near the top of his high school class, with high SAT scores and an attractive set of choices for where to attend college. Many of the students on campus were happy to be there for what the school had to offer them. But given its rather small size and the fact that it was not one of the Ivy League schools, someone like Edward, with presumably a strong academic background, very well may have chosen it so he could be the big fish in a little pond rather than a small fish in a prestigious top-notch institution. I suspected that was the case.

The early signs of being a Meanderer were evident when Edward was in college. Along with many of his classmates, he was on the path to med school, but before graduating, he'd changed his mind. Now orienting himself toward a graduate program in geology, he had had to spend a couple of years after graduation beefing up his credentials. To be clear, switching majors and taking a few years to prep for grad school isn't in and of itself diagnostic of a weak identity, but since we have the benefit of hindsight, this first career switch foretold his many later vacillations.

After Edward earned his doctoral degree, he took a job for a few years as a geologist for a mining company, a position that seemed quite fitting given his graduate training. But a few years later, something caused him to switch gears yet again and enter career number three: teaching English as a second language at a community college. So now you might think that he, having left geology behind, would have stuck with the teaching job for at least a few years, but this was not to be. The teaching was only a way station before he was on the job hunt again, spending one year as an accountant and then, shortly after that, back around to geology, career number two (or number five, depending on how you count it).

By this time, Edward was getting a bit long in the tooth for an entry-level position, all that he would qualify for given his relative lack of experience as a working geologist. If he was going to make it in the profession, he'd have to settle for something at low pay and would most likely have to move to wherever the jobs were available. He also would be expected to produce letters of reference from previous employers familiar with his work as a geologist, not as a teacher or an accountant. Although he didn't know it at the time, success was starting to slip away from Edward's grasp. Instead of getting a job in his field at a major company, he decided to go back to teaching, settling for a post teaching a general survey course on environmental science at a community college. He probably attracted a great deal of favorable attention because, as scattered as his background was, he was still overqualified for the job. My guess is that he was the best thing to happen to the teaching of introductory courses for quite some time in a small and overworked department.

In the midst of all this career turmoil, Edward went through a series of brief cohabitations, none of which led to a lasting relationship. It was impossible for me to know much about any of these partners, but it seemed pretty clear from what I did know about Edward that his inability to make career commitments spilled over into his ability to maintain emotional commitments. People who are low on identity, as Edward was, are also low on intimacy, because making commitments to a partner requires having solid knowledge of who you are. During much of his life, his intimacy scores were, in fact, lower than those of his peers. His many partners may have left him out of frustration due to his constant meandering and his topsy-turvy lifestyle.

Though Edward's life was deviating further and further from its promising beginnings, he may have continued to believe that it was just a matter of time before things would turn around. He likely entered each new career choice with the fervent belief that this time it would be the "one." But each change made success even more elusive.

Being successful, talented, or blessed with good fortune early in life, though helpful for many in getting their start, can also become a curse. If you have these strengths in youth but don't follow up by continuing to develop and apply yourself to maintain and grow them, you run the risk of never realizing your potential. I see someone like Edward as having formed an identity in high school and college as a star achiever, but as his life continued to go off course, he never adjusted his identity accordingly. When he couldn't follow through on any one set of commitments, the reality was that he was becoming a failure. Then, to protect himself from the anxiety of facing his failure, he had no choice but to seek alternative sources of self-esteem. Like the Wizard of Oz, people like Edward build up a smoke screen to reinforce for the benefit of themselves and others the image of their own importance. But their friends and family members may not be so easily fooled. If you know anyone like this, chances are good that you want to jostle them and bring them back to reality.

But just as it's not always prudent to wake a sleepwalker, it could be better to let the Edwards of the world continue to live out their small fantasies. After all, they are not causing harm. Why not let him live out his belief that he is making a difference in the world at large? I would say "sure" were it not for three crucial factors: One is the very sad and unnecessary loss of potential that Edward represents. When you see a brilliant mind gone so awry, you probably, like me, feel saddened by the waste. Second, the "sleepwalker" might wake up on his own one day. Then he will fall, and fall hard. Helping him reach consciousness slowly and in a way that does not bruise his ego too harshly can allow him to shed the aura of his false identity and take on the more authentic, but flawed, view of himself as a man in need of worthwhile enterprise. If you're an Edward, or know one, the dawning of this realization can be therapeutic, especially when there's still time to change.

Which brings me to my third point: Edward still has time to fix some of the problems in his life—he could still teach or he could find employment in some capacity that uses his many areas of expertise. He does have the opportunity to look back on his accomplishments ten or fifteen years from now and feel that his life has amounted to more than random wandering. It is not unrealistic for a Meanderer to settle down in one place, with proper guidance.

In describing the identity crisis, Erikson focused on development during the years of adolescence and young adulthood but didn't explore what might happen later in life. His assumption, along with the researchers who would eventually continue to test his theory on college students, was that once people attained their identities in adolescence, it would remain more or less steady in the following decades, barring an unforeseen derailment. In other words, if you had an identity crisis in your teens, it was enough to rate you as a person who had truly "achieved" an identity, even if you hadn't reexamined alternatives in years. Similarly, people who did not achieve an identity in adolescence were thought to lack a clear sense of self throughout their lives. My position on this, and I have the data to support it, is that coming to grips with your identity is a lifelong process. Although adolescence is an important time for identity formation, the questions about who we are do not stop then. Our identities can change, and chances to question our commitments can come along throughout life.

The Meandering Way includes people who once had a coherent identity when they were younger and those who did not. What they have in common is that their adult years are being frittered away as they question each step they take and fail to settle on one clear life plan. Or worse yet, they have given up on realizing their earlier hopes and dreams entirely because they have lost conviction in their own ability to realize their potential.

Julia

Julia's life story is a very sad, if not tragic, illustration of how potential can be lost when people fail to develop a cohesive identity and at the same time are the victims of an unsupportive environment. Starting with the basic data from her questionnaires, the trajectory of her identity scores resembled an inverted *U,* with increases during her forties followed by a rapid descent while she was in her fifties. Her other scores also dipped precipitously, including her overall life satisfaction.

The evidence from her work history showed me that she was a brilliant student during her college days. Right after graduation she was accepted into one of the best doctoral programs in the United States, at a prestigious university in New England. After completing her doctorate in just four short years—unusual for someone studying Greek antiquity— she landed an assistant professorship at an outstanding school in the Midwest. She was on track to win tenure, the academic Holy Grail, had she been able to pass further muster. Therein lay the problem.

You've probably heard the phrase "publish or perish" as the motto of academic teaching posts. No matter what their field of study, professors are expected to do research and teach, serve on committees, supervise students, attend conferences, and on and on and on. When we sign on for these jobs, we know the drill. On the flip side of the pressures, there are many benefits that come with these positions, particularly academic freedom, should we agree to meet these obligations. (I wanted to mention the upside of academia, lest you think I'm complaining about my own job!) In fact, I've often thought that the system, though potentially a cruel one, is very explicit in its demands. Those who don't make tenure usually don't fail to do so because they lack knowledge about the hurdles that need to be jumped over.

There is one legitimate problem, though, that afflicts many people starting out in this career track: The "publish" part of the equation is weighted most heavily, even though there are many other competing demands put on young professors. They are given heavy teaching loads with new courses to prepare. Of course, students gravitate to young professors because they are closer to them in age than senior faculty. These student visits amount to a considerable, though often pleasurable, time burden. It's hard to shut the door on an eager undergrad hoping to learn more about the subject matter that you yourself find so fascinating.

So now let's get back to Julia, trying to navigate these rough waters. I know from my own experience that the only way that she could have managed to fulfill all of these expectations in the course of a normal work day was by beginning at six A.M. and keeping going until ten or eleven at night (at least). I haven't even mentioned that she most likely would have been expected to seek funding for her research, which undoubtedly was expensive to conduct, given that she was pursuing the study of ancient Greek manuscripts. More than that, her colleagues in the department had international reputations, and many had received prestigious awards such as Guggenheims and Fulbrights. They were funding their own research and probably thought she should, too.

Looking at Julia's work history data from her surveys, I could only conclude that she spent the seven years needed to be considered for tenure but then ultimately failed to make the grade. I found her dissertation through online library resources, but no amount of scouring in my university's library catalog could produce evidence that she had written even a single article. I found only one citation to her work in someone else's book on the same rather arcane topic—again, a bad sign for her productivity levels. Then, examining her identity scores at that time, which were on their way up, I couldn't attribute the cause of her failure in this situation to a delayed identity crisis. No, that crisis was to come in her fifties, when she was dealing with the reality of a different issue— the clear evidence that she would not and could not hope to live up to her early promise and use her education in productive ways. But I'll return to that later.

One night while waiting for a long-delayed flight at O'Hare airport, I was working on Julia's data, and as the hour got later, I let my imagination wander as I tried to envision the scene when her department chair would have dropped the bombshell on Julia that her chances of getting tenure were dismal. Maybe I was doing a bit of projecting from my own experience of pre-tenure evaluation, which was taking place at about the same time Julia's was, in the late 1970s (but fortunately with more success). Julia would most likely have received a cordial, though to her probably ominous, invitation from the dean's secretary to make an appointment with the big boss. If she had any self-insight, Julia would have realized that this was going to be one of the more uncomfortable hours of her life. I imagine her heart sank as she realized that her academic career was reaching its finale. Without any publications and having been denied tenure in this, her first job, she would not be able to land a new post in the competitive world of academia.

As I imagined this scenario, I felt myself getting annoyed by the lack of mentoring Julia received. Surely someone could have helped this bright young scholar avoid total career implosion by giving her some kindly advice on the perils of not publishing. Not even her grad school professor seemed to have offered her some concrete assistance by co-authoring a book or article with her.

Now, back in the general job market, her Ph.D. would be more of a handicap than an advantage. Few people outside academia want to hire a person who is overqualified, and by this time, Julia wouldn't have seen much point in using her degree to win a high-paying or prestigious job. In fact, from her job title it was pretty evident that she had taken the first paid position she could find, which turned out to be as an office clerk in the administration of a small local township. Perhaps she liked the fact that, though low-paying, it was nine to five and involved no fruitlessly spent nights or weekends trying to keep up with a crushing workload of extra research, paper grading, or committee responsibilities.

So, if you weren't reading about Julia in this chapter on the Meandering Way, you might be hoping (as I was) that the story would have a better outcome. Unfortunately, it doesn't. More than twenty years later, she was at the same job level, still lacking a clear sense of self-confidence or passion toward her commitments. In the process of searching for new information about her, I spotted her in various nooks and crannies of the Web as someone who enjoys Italian wine and various quasi-academic pursuits such as getting together with friends and planning educational trips to Europe and Asia. As engaging as these interests might be, however, she nevertheless cannot help but be reminded on a daily basis of what she could have been had she used her intellectual talents to their fullest capacity to advance the study of the classics.

As we see from Edward and Julia, being smart early in life is not enough to guarantee success later on, and in fact academic "smarts" may get in the way. Tufts University psychologist Robert Sternberg talks about "successful intelligence," which allows us to negotiate the practical challenges of daily life. I would say that in addition to knowing how to apply your intelligence to commonsense problems, you also need to know where you are headed in your life pursuits. And knowing where you want to go early is not enough to sustain you throughout your middle and later years. The self-insight needed to keep you feeling fulfilled requires vigilance to ensure that you are making the best use of your intelligence.

Julia's story also shows the importance of being mentored during the stressful early years of one's career. As someone who received this benefit in my twenties, I know how crucial this support can prove to be.

It's something all of us mid-lifers should keep in mind when we interact with our young colleagues.

Alan

To explain more about the connection between maturity and identity formation, I'm going to tell you next about Alan's life. He was another character whose story defied common sense. He didn't fall short of expectations to the same extent that Edward and Julia did, but I would not consider him a happy man by any stretch of the imagination.

Although he wasn't in bad shape in terms of his identity during college, by his twenties, Alan's scores started to plummet. It was pretty easy for me to piece together his life story because many of his exploits were posted on the Web, showing that his interests were, to put a positive spin on it, "wide-ranging." But if you were being realistic, you would call them "unfocused." What didn't pop up in my Internet searches was what I knew from the private questionnaires he sent to me, which revealed the inner life of a man who was, as the song goes, looking for love in all the wrong places. He couldn't seem to commit to a long-term relationship, and even though his intimacy scores wavered around the mid to low end of the continuum of people in my sample, the fundamental problem seemed to be one of coming to grips with his own self-definition. Hence his inability to commit to a relationship.

In college Alan wasn't necessarily the most highly motivated person in his class, but he was by no means the least. His work ethic was on the low side, but his identity was about in the middle range for my sample. Like Julia, he went on to get a graduate degree, which he finished in close to record time. Another brilliant scholar off to a fiery start. With his doctorate in hand, a career in aeronautical engineering seemed certain.

By his late twenties Alan was reaping the benefits of having gotten ahead of his peers and was well rewarded in terms of salary and promotions. But his scores told me that there must have been some twinges of self-doubt starting to creep into his view of himself. By his early thirties, his identity scores were far lower than those of my other sample participants, most of whom had shot up from their college days into the high and positive range. My guess is that as a result of rushing through his early training so quickly, he was starting to question whether he'd actually taken the right path. Perhaps he wondered if he should have pursued his artistic side, which in his forties was starting to show—he had work on display in several publicized sculpture exhibits.

The discontent that Alan was starting to experience at work seemed to take its toll on his home life. By his midthirties he was done with his first marriage. Soon after it ended, he was on to his second wife, this time in a seemingly more promising way. Their marriage was to last nearly two decades. However, his lack of a clear-cut direction was about to spill over into his second marriage, as I learned when he completed the questionnaires in his fifties. This second marriage was now clearly doomed. Someone who was basically optimistic if not content, Alan entered into his third marriage several years before my last round of testing.

Alan's choice of a wife the third time around was a bit surprising to me. There he was, highly educated and employed in a well-respected occupation in which the norm would be to marry a woman close to his own educational background and prestige level. Alan broke out of the norm for someone in his social circle and moved in with a woman with only a high school degree, one of a handful not to attend college in this relatively well-educated sample. Her job as a sales assistant in a discount shoe store also diverged rather considerably from those of the other partners and spouses. It was hard for me to see, on the basis of this factual data alone, what the two had in common. I supposed that Alan may have viewed her as a refreshing change from the people he had associated with for most of his adult life. Unfortunately, this choice did not seem to be working, as Alan's overall satisfaction was as low as it had ever been.

Unlike Edward and Julia, Alan had a relatively stable career path, and it was only in his relationships that the meandering seemed to express itself. However, his career stability was not accompanied by a solid sense of identity or feelings of fulfillment, and it was for these reasons that I classified him on this pathway. I had a few other clues that reinforced my interpretation of Alan's life story. He'd received a few awards within his community for serving as a mentor to a high school senior interested in engineering. So at least he was able to achieve some success outside of his normal everyday work routines. In trying to get at the root of Alan's identity problems, I tried to come to an understanding of why his identity had taken such a downward turn in his middle years and was so much lower than that of his peers. Perhaps he regretted never exploring various facets of his career and other interests. Now, nearing the age of sixty, he likely wishes that he could have broken the mold a little sooner and pursued relationships and interests that would have allowed him more freedom of self-expression. If he had explored those alternatives when he was younger, perhaps he wouldn't have found himself so frustrated with the choices he settled down to make so quickly and, I would venture to say in retrospect, so rashly.

When Erikson talked about the search for identity, he at one point used the term "moratorium" to refer to the psychological state of not making any decisions—in other words, putting a ban on making a commitment. One result of this process might be a state of identity diffuseness, the problem that seemed to characterize Edward as he drifted from job to job. Julia's problems were similar in nature, though she didn't so much drift as fail to actualize her intellectual potential. She probably would have been content to remain in her academic job had she just been able to figure out the magic formula a little earlier. As far as Alan was concerned, a bit more exploration when he was younger might have served to prevent the identity crisis he would come to experience only when he thought it was too late to experiment.

Janet

So far we have seen the Meandering Way expressed as vacillations in career choices, failure to realize potential, and feelings of identity malaise. Now we encounter Janet, another brilliant person, whose life took even wider swings, accompanied by huge shifts in her personality scores. Janet seemed to be in a permanent state of crisis throughout her life; in fact, she wasn't merely meandering, she was careening.

On the face of it, piecing together Janet's story wasn't difficult. Like many of the volunteers in my study, she was a loyal participant who not only completed each of the testings but also provided me with extensive details about each of her many shifting commitments, career and otherwise.

Though her identity scores were never particularly high, she did achieve a peak of sorts in her forties. Unfortunately, it was only a temporary upswing. By the time she was in her midfifties, her identity had once again plummeted downward. Corresponding to this unfortunate trajectory was a series of truly radical career changes. Janet's meandering occurred both within her own sense of self and in her outward adaptation to the world of work.

Like the other three sample members that I've described who are on this pathway, Janet was off to a brilliant start in life. She progressed readily through law school, passed the bar, and established herself as an assistant district attorney. In the midst of her career ascendancy, she married a man with professional credentials close to her own and, unlike Alan's current spouse, very consistent with those of others in the sample. When Janet checked in with me in the late 1970s, all seemed to be going relatively well for this thirtysomething star on the rise, aside from her lower-than-average identity scale score.

By her forties, Janet was still involved in the legal profession, but there was a troubling sign on the horizon. For a brief period, not corresponding to anything I could pinpoint, she had taken a job as an office clerk. What was going on? She clearly hadn't needed the extra cash, or so it would have seemed, given her professional training. Had she been disbarred? Did she just decide to hang up her career for a while to allow her to take stock of her life? Even more puzzling was that her identity score, in fact, was the highest it was ever to be, so I doubted she was having something like a full-blown crisis. At the time, I could only conclude that she had done something to get herself fired from her job, derailing her from her upward career trajectory.

However, that analysis seemed to be contradicted by what was to follow in her early fifties. Shortly after the third follow-up test was completed, she again took up clerical work, this time for a full two years. A stint in Europe in a legal clinic was followed by an even more radical career departure to a job as a mail clerk in the local branch of a large company. Then, even more surprising—she enrolled in a dental hygienist training program.

Now, after reversing that career choice, she is back where she started, working in the field of criminal law as a public defender in a small town in Ohio. Occasionally she writes brief articles in various law review journals and even coauthors papers in a legal studies publication every now and then, so she seems to maintain her professional connections.

The most likely conclusion that I arrived at after analyzing information I had about her and carefully scrutinizing her scores is that she simply wanted out of the field of law while she explored these other options. Then she gravitated back to her original passion. I ended up putting her in the category of the Meandering Way rather than the Downward Slope, because unlike people on the Downward Slope, she wasn't actually shooting herself in the foot (a pattern you will see later in the book). She seemed to be able to hop back onto her professional career path without suffering undue harm.

Other than the damage wrought on her own psyche, there was also the waste of potential that resulted from this apparently well-intentioned but misguided soul frittering away her time on this planet. How much could she have helped others if she'd figured out her own life's direction rather than devoting her intellectual and professional energies to deciding whether a package had the right postage or account code?

There is nothing inherently troubling or unusual about a college-educated person filling a low-paying job that does not require a college education. The problem, at least for Janet, was that her advanced professional training was not being used to its fullest capacity. People can make important contributions to the world no matter what their occupation is (see Chapter 11). The issue here is whether you are living up to your fullest potential. This was the crux of Janet's dilemma.

If ever there was an example of a person in a prolonged period of identity exploration, it was Janet. It is one thing to be open to alternatives but quite another to spend all of your adult years questioning and challenging your commitments and purpose in life. When you reach your fifties and you realize that many options are getting less and less viable, the letdown can be harsh indeed.

ACTION PLAN

How to Get Off the Meandering Way

As you've seen in the stories of my sample participants who have taken the Meandering Way, they were unable to actualize their early life potential because they could not focus their abilities on a definite set of commitments. As a result, they have ended up wandering without direction or purpose. When people question their identities in youth, they are allowed a certain amount of time and freedom to explore various commitments, and if this goes on for only a few years, it is no harm, no foul. When it goes on for decades, the lack of direction takes its toll. Time runs out, and as people get older, each of their new explorations becomes more and more costly because there is more at stake. They can no longer afford that feeling of invulnerability that pervades the mentality of many young people.

Some people on the Meandering Way seem to fit the Peter Pan mold. As the song goes, they just "won't grow up." This is a key feature of the mentality of people on this pathway. Eternally waiting for a ship to come in that never does, they believe that if they just turn this way or that way, the success and clarity of self-definition they seek will all of a sudden emerge.

Unaware of or unconcerned about the passage of time, they incorrectly see their opportunities to make change as limitless.

Unfortunately, as the years go by and their success continues to elude them, their self-estimation does not change accordingly. Ironically, their early success becomes not the foundation for later accomplishments but instead the basis for a view of the self that continues to diverge further and further away from the reality of their failures.

So, what can you do if you are a Meanderer and want to move to a pathway that will lead to greater self-clarification? Pointing out now that your lack of direction caused you to flounder will not be particularly beneficial. You can't erase the passage of the years or recapture your earlier promise. We have to start by helping you reconnect with the core of your sense of self by asking some basic questions: What were your original goals in life? What made you deviate from pursuing those goals? What frightened you about making commitments? What makes you feel that you are out of touch with your real sense of purpose?

The U.S. Census tells us that a surprisingly large percentage, something like 40 percent, of people age fifty-one to sixty-five are involved in adult education. But the reality of making a complete turnabout in your late fifties is a bit daunting. If you are on the Meandering Way, I would encourage you to look at what you have most enjoyed and been successful at and use that as a way to strengthen your inner sense of accomplishment.

If you find yourself on the Meandering Way, you may be living out the myth that there is always something better around the corner and that if you could just find it, you'd be happy. If you can dissuade yourself from this illusion and allow yourself to see that more than likely you've done what you've done because it did provide you with fulfillment, it might allow you to appreciate the commitments you've already made. It may be true that objectively speaking you have not utilized your talents to the fullest, but since we can't turn the clock back, you can instead reframe what you have been successful at in a more positive light.

Having established a firmer internal base within yourself, you can now look at the future with less panic and perhaps with more confidence in the decisions you have made in the past. Then you can make a commitment to some variant of what is most central to your sense of self and start to carry it out. Focusing your energy on one set of pursuits and seeing yourself as successful in those pursuits will allow you to experience the type of fulfillment that comes to those on the Authentic Road. If nothing else, you have shown that you are flexible and open to considering alternatives rather than being rigidly opposed to change. You have developed a wide variety of skills as you have pursued your divergent interests. If you can rein in that flexibility and focus your energies, you will be able to spend the rest of your life enjoying the sense of inner accomplishment that comes from following through on your passions.

CHAPTER 6

The Straight and Narrow Way

For some people, the years pass in a remarkably consistent fashion. These people stay in the same community, perhaps even the same house, for decades if not half centuries. While they and their families get older, the passing years produce little in the way of personal changes. Perhaps they climb up the rungs of their career ladders, but they don't shift psychological gears along the way. These are the people whose annual holiday letters change very little; you could probably write them yourself just by switching in their latest vacation spot. Call them at ten A.M. on a Saturday and they will be doing exactly what they did at ten A.M. on a Saturday ten, twenty, or thirty years ago.

Although the superficial appearance of continuity isn't always indicative of what's going on inside, there is a sense that those on the Straight and Narrow Way avoid change at all levels as much as possible. When forced to do so, they may upgrade their computers or cellphones, but they'll grumble constantly that they liked the old ones better because they were used to them. I think about some of the men I see at meetings from year to year, wearing the same clothes they wore as young men— be it navy-blue blazers and khaki pants or T-shirts and jeans. The women style their hair the same way they did as young adults, even as that hair gets grayer and grayer. In a way it's kind of reassuring to see these bastions of stability—we know what to expect from them. On the other hand, it's a little saddening, at least to me, to think that people can be so resistant to feedback from the outside world.

These are just the outside trappings of the Straight and Narrow Way. Of course, there is more going on beneath the surface. Now we'll go more in depth to understand why people follow this pathway and what happens to them when they do.

When I was examining people's life pathways for one of the early studies I completed with this sample, it was pretty easy to spot these stable folks and put them into a category. They were the ones who stayed in the same relationship, often since college graduation, and who stayed in the same career or job from their college years to the present. I mentioned how tedious the coding process could become for people on the Meandering Way because of the many changes that had to be entered into the data, so I have to admit that I was always happy when I identified a stable participant, because it meant I could get through the coding quickly, and move on to the set of questionnaires.

However, pretty soon I found myself getting pretty bored and sort of scared by these superstable people. At times I thought that maybe they had something over me because my life hadn't been that stable. They had avoided some of the traps that I'd fallen into in my early adult years. But as I scored their personality questionnaires, I realized that maybe they weren't so well-off after all. Stability has its seductive features, especially when people in its clutches look at the way others who embrace change can sometimes fall flat on their faces. And yes, it's true that some of the stable people received favorable personality scores, but on average, theirs were lower than those of people who were more open to a little adventure.

It is also important to mention that the people on this pathway are unlikely to be tremendously reflective or insightful. When you ask people who don't engage in self-scrutiny whether or not they spend time examining themselves or their lives, they tend to say they do. Almost everyone likes to say that they are flexible and open, because these qualities are so highly valued in our current social climate. Many people also like to say that they are happy. Surveys show that the average person tends to report levels of happiness higher than the theoretical "average person." These problems get in the way of any research based on self-report, but they present a particular challenge when examining the lives of people who shove their insecurities and fears under the rug, the well-known defense mechanism of denial. People deny that they are in denial. On the basis of the relatively low ego integrity scores the people on the Straight and Narrow Way received in my study, I would have to assume that there is more inner angst going on with these people than they admit.

Bruce

At the outset of the book, I introduced you to one of the participants on the Straight and Narrow Way, Albert—an orthodontist who followed a straight line from his college days to the present, never looking left or right, only to suffer in midlife from deep-seated unhappiness. Now I'd like you to meet his kindred spirit, Bruce. Scoring Bruce's life history questionnaire took a suspiciously short amount of time. I wondered whether his personality scores would echo the restricted route of his life choices.

Unlike his classmates, Bruce took his studies very seriously. He was not one of those students hanging around his dorm room drinking or taking drugs; nor was he out there in the quad protesting the war. Because I knew that he would eventually receive a graduate degree in bio-statistics, it didn't surprise me to see that he was one of the more studious people in the sample. Maybe he was one of those science types who wasn't ashamed to wear a plastic pencil protector in his shirt pocket. Maybe he even took pride in that testimony to his future professional exploits. The other studious young men in his class may have been preparing for more lucrative careers in medicine or law, but Bruce seemed to feel okay about where he was heading.

A deeper look at Bruce's psychological portrait from his college days revealed that in contrast to the clarity of his career choice, he was not completely ready for a long-term relationship, at least as judged by his low scores on Erikson's quality of intimacy. It surprised me, then, to see that he had moved in with his girlfriend shortly after college graduation and remained with her until their marriage several years later. I would have predicted that Bruce would spend more time as a loner before getting involved in a relationship. I wondered if he did so because it was what would have been expected of someone in his social circle. With such low intimacy scores, feeling comfortable in a close relationship might have been a problem for him. On the other hand, it's possible that this relationship protected him from even more inner loneliness.

Career-wise, by his midtwenties, Bruce was already well ensconced in the agency where he would work for his adult life. I assume this was a position he wanted, because it fit so closely with his training. Soon he began to work his way up the ranks in a small government commission that investigated outbreaks of infectious diseases. In this starter job, he was sent out to locations where he completed his analyses on the spot. The travel would certainly be tiring, but the work allowed him to apply his training to real-life situations in the field. During that time, his personality was developing in some of Erikson's lower-order stages, which had been low when Bruce was in college. By the time Bruce was thirty-one, he was a well-rounded young man in reasonably good shape, apart from his weakness in the area of intimacy.

When Bruce filled out his surveys again in his forties, they revealed that he was beginning to burn out a little bit. I could see that his work ethic wasn't quite as strong as it had been; nor was it as strong as those of his fellow mid-lifers. Were the edges of that early career commitment wearing thin? Perhaps he was disappointed that he hadn't received a real promotion in almost ten years and didn't see much room for advancement. On the other hand, his salary and benefits were probably good enough to keep him from aggressively looking elsewhere. And so he was, realistically or unrealistically, feeling rather stuck.

Most of the study participants were stable on the quality of initiative, unless something drastic had occurred to them to shake them up and send them in the opposite direction. In Bruce's case, though his life appeared the same, this was an area that took a huge dip. The stability that characterized Bruce's life began to take its toll on his ability to use his imagination, and maybe to relax and kick up his heels a little bit—to take a break from his life of toiling in the trenches.

In fact, although Bruce's level of initiative was the most significant victim of his unswerving lifestyle, he was taking hits across the board. Most distressing was his admission that he didn't feel satisfied with his life choices, as reflected in his low ego integrity and life satisfaction scores. How ironic to have devoted himself so thoroughly to his life of public service only to now feel, as he reached what should have been the pinnacle of his achievements (he was finally promoted), that his efforts were not making a difference in the world.

About two years after completing my last set of questionnaires, my online research showed that Bruce was assigned to investigate a cholera epidemic in Africa that had inflicted a heavy death toll, particularly affecting children. I wondered whether he had the psychological resources to handle what must have been a tremendously upsetting and emotionally draining experience. On the other hand, given his professional training and the lack of strong evidence that there was an empathic streak in his personality, it is likely that he approached the gruesome task without a great deal of personal involvement. Time will tell whether this experience further eroded his already low feelings of fulfillment or whether it was just one more investigation that didn't take its psychological toll.

The straight and steady life path that Bruce took is one that characterizes a number of people in my study. Many of them, like Bruce, felt unfulfilled after spending thirty years carrying out essentially the same day-to-day existence. As they reached their late fifties, the dissatisfaction cracked the surface of a veneer of success.

Janice

Janice is our next traveler on the Straight and Narrow Way, but in comparison to Bruce, she seems to have done very well for herself in her personal life and her career. In fact, when I opened Janet's most recently filled-out questionnaires, I was struck by the contrast between her impressive achievements and her low life-satisfaction rating. It was the lowest possible on the scale. I set about trying to uncover the reasons for this paradox of her life. A successful administrator of a major recycling firm, Janice had slogged her way through a male-dominated profession at a time when women were only just being let into the exclusive boys' clubs of the upper managerial brackets of the corporate world. Scanning her work and family history, I couldn't see anything that she should have been ashamed of or unhappy about.

I would have to keep digging to unravel Janice's mysterious personality development. Back in college, her highest scores were on the scale measuring autonomy. She was an independent soul. Her identity score, on the other hand, was far below average. Autonomous but low in identity? It didn't quite fit. Some of her other scores were also on the low side compared with her peers. So it seemed as though she faced a number of significant challenges that would ultimately have a negative effect on her well-being.

Janice left out a few pieces of her work and educational history when she filled out her second survey at the age of thirty-one. She reported taking part-time courses in French literature at a local college, probably to satisfy her avocational interests. But before long, she was embarking on the career where she would remain for the next thirty years. Technically, she might not have been as straight and narrow as Bruce, but her job history was still remarkably consistent.

Her romantic involvements were also stable. From college graduation on, she cohabitated with a female partner, a union that set her apart from the norms of the era. By her early thirties, Janice had the highest scores she would receive throughout the study, perhaps reflecting that she was well on her way toward realizing both her occupational and her emotional dreams.

But the bubble burst when she was in her forties, and she kept on going downward, to reach the lowest point in the most recent survey, which she filled out in her late fifties. She had very few positive things to say about herself this time around. She described herself as inauthentic, restrained, self-preoccupied, spread too thin, pessimistic, uncomfortable around others, preoccupied with her failures, and afraid of getting old.

It's a story that repeats itself throughout my study, unfortunately: An outwardly successful professional has an unrewarding and dismal internal life. I tried to visualize what in her life could be causing so much turmoil. Perhaps Janice didn't feel as though she was making enough of a difference in the world at large. She described herself as interested in learning and concerned about others, and her job just might not have been cutting it for her. Close relationships seemed to be her forte, and in fact, her highest score was on the intimacy scale.

If I had to pinpoint Janice's problem, it would be that she felt her career was unrewarding and that she believed she had made the wrong decision when she'd decided to cast her fate in the arena of industry instead of following her heart and going into the arts. Perhaps it's the money that keeps her in the field and inhibits her from seeking greater congruence between expression of her true self and the world of industrial waste she inhabits in her work. Janice would be an excellent candidate for rehabilitation to help her find her way to the Authentic Road if she follows the Action Plan for the Straight and Narrow Way.

Herb

Along the Straight and Narrow Way we also find Herb, a supervisor in a chemical engineering firm who, though he's moved up in the ranks, has remained in the same basic position his whole working life. Apart from his job duties, however, Herb has been an avid computer techie and to this day is an active participant in Internet groups dealing with highly complex and somewhat arcane computer programming issues that, quite frankly, I cannot even begin to comprehend.

A couple of years ago, when searching for an address update, I inadvertently found myself viewing some of his conversations online, archived on a public message board. These exchanges seemed to be on the friendly side, though dry and technical. In preparing his story, I went back to the same source, where more recent conversations appeared, and saw that his tone was getting a bit grumpier.

All of this is to set the stage for the story of a participant who started out in college in pretty good shape, psychologically speaking. His scores were good, except on the quality of industry, which was low, even for his era. So when his questionnaires arrived during his early thirties, I wasn't expecting to see that half of his other scores had taken a nosedive, while his industry levels had increased substantially. He seemed to be lagging in areas where his fellow thirtysomethings were growing by leaps and bounds, particularly identity and intimacy. The pattern would continue through his fifties, when Herb emerged as the very lowest of the group in ego integrity, and was also low in trust. What occurred between his forties and fifties to make him become so embittered?

In studying this sad and rather unusual pattern, I sensed that it marked nothing short of a psychosocial meltdown, one that I probably would not have predicted on the basis of his early adult scores alone. But as I thought about his case, I was reminded of a colleague of mine at another university who similarly became addicted to the esoteric aspects of computer programming. I would hear from him once in a while over the years, when he would tell me about his recent work. Though in his eyes the research was important and groundbreaking, I wondered about its ultimate value. He hadn't received many accolades or even the most minimal recognition from his professional societies. I got the impression that, for the most part, he did nothing more than tinker endlessly with programs that seemed to have very little application outside the narrow confines of a small group of methodologists who spent years coming up with ways to count and score miniscule atoms of body language in videotaped interactions. Maybe this was what Herb's life was like: spending years working in a small but ultimately unproductive venture, collaborating with like-minded colleagues who themselves had been spinning their wheels for years in virtual obscurity. Though science can be a lonely profession at times, Herb might be one of those people who substitutes his online community for one made of flesh and blood.

Can Herb avoid staying on the Straight and Narrow Way that led him to suffer such an unhappy course? As you'll see later, moving off this pathway is indeed possible. I would suggest that Herb put aside his intellectual pursuits for a while and seek more emotionally fulfilling ways to interact with the people in his life. Perhaps he could balance his involvement in research with a hobby that would provide him with a way to be more physically active. Or how about sharing his skills in the area of programming with high school kids or teaching an evening or online course at a local community college? The point would be to get out of what clearly for him is a lonely and unrewarding rut.

I almost dread seeing what Herb will look like in the next round of testing because the situation right now looks so dire. However, I hope I will be surprised and find out that someone or something has inspired him to explore some alternatives, get more involved in the outside world, and in the process become more accepting of himself and his life so far.

Claire

We'll now return to Claire, whom I mentioned briefly in Chapter 1. Like Janice, Claire didn't settle into a single path after college graduation. But it wasn't long before she did, and she still remains in that path today. She married right after college graduation and is now a mother of two. While her husband started dental school, she completed a master's in educational administration.

But Claire was never to use her master's degree, because just as with many other women of her generation, she set it aside to raise her children. The employment she listed in her questionnaires showed her as a volunteer for her local hospital, the same one in which her mother had been involved.

From comparing Claire to her mother, I came up with the hunch that Claire's identity was forged by her desire to emulate her mother, a woman who had gained a great deal of respect in the community and perhaps enjoyed seeing her daughter follow in her noble footsteps. Though the work Claire did contributed in important ways to her community, I had reason to believe it was not the way she ultimately would have liked to use her talents.

It took a number of years for this dissatisfaction to express itself. In college, she was low in trust, autonomy, identity, and intimacy (i.e., four out of six scales). Almost everything improved by her early thirties, just after she had started her family. But at the same time, her initiative scores dipped precipitously. Perhaps she was feeling constrained as she entered grownup life. Maybe her low scores in college reflected rebellion on her part or perhaps she was just plain depressed. In any case, her trip down the Straight and Narrow Way was confirmed.

As a side note, Claire's case shows us why it's useful to examine development over time. If we had looked at only her college scores, we wouldn't have seen how her identity and other key features of her personality evolved over time.

Unfortunately, Claire didn't send back her questionnaires when she was in her forties. But if we map her trajectory straight from her thirties to her fifties, we see only one discernible blip, and that is a decrease in ego integrity. Claire was doing pretty well except in her feelings of acceptance of her past life decisions. Was she regretting not having used her education? Her life satisfaction was also lower than the other people in my sample. Now that her kids were out of the house, perhaps Claire was wondering whether she'd made the right choices after all, especially because she was probably seeing other women her age reaping the benefits of having remained active in their careers. It might be hard to motivate someone like Claire to make a switch from the Straight and Narrow Way because she seems to be living a comfortable, if predictable and unsatisfying, life. She remains a pillar of her community and seems to have accumulated a great deal of respect as a result, but with so many low points in her personality profile, it's an existence that will ultimately fall short of providing her with true fulfillment.

ACTION PLAN

Shaking Up the Straight and Narrow Way

The desire for sameness and repetition seems to lead to a sort of motivational inertia for people who remain on the Straight and Narrow Way. Anxiety about change and a belief that the old ways were preferable play out in this group's general resistance to change and tendency at times to identify with members of older generations. Many of those who are on the Straight and Narrow Way are leading the lives that were set for them by parents who explicitly or implicitly directed their choices of careers, values, and even life partners.

What prevents people on this pathway from being more flexible? When I first came across them in my sample, I was reminded of the concept of the "foreclosed identity" introduced by psychologist James Marcia in his studies of identity in adolescents. He proposed the radical but now accepted idea that it is possible for adolescents to arrive at a firm identity without actually experiencing an identity crisis. Similarly, those in the Straight and Narrow Way maintain their commitments through life without going through serious evaluation on a regular, or even occasional, basis. Unfortunately, they are setting themselves up to find at some point along the way that the commitments resulting from those early decisions are wearing thin. And if something happens unexpectedly that threatens the status quo, they are not resilient enough to be able to adapt to it without a great deal of anguish. Losing their job, having a spouse cheat on them, seeing some of their cherished youthful prowess dwindle, or being challenged by a rebellious teenage kid can cause their fragile outward coating to break and can expose their weak interior, much like what happens if you touch a chocolate-covered marshmallow too hard.

There's another angle to the Straight and Narrow Way as well, and it has to do with our willingness to gamble on a risky choice. Psychologists have found that we are more conservative when we think we are ahead and more likely to take a chance when we think we are losing. People on the Straight and Narrow Way often have very comfortable—and in some ways "satisfactory," if not satisfied—lives. The longer they remain at that comfort level, the harder it is for them to contemplate making a change in that nice life. The danger is that as the years go by, they will remain comfortable but never reach inner fulfillment.

The Straight and Narrow Way, then, has its enticements, because even if a person is unhappy, at least there is some predictability to the unhappiness. Its dangers may be difficult to appreciate for people who sometimes ache for sameness and continuity, but for those who are stuck on this path, relief from personality doldrums or worse can come only from stretching themselves and experimenting.

In some cases, even bad changes can be preferable to no changes, because at least those catapult people out of their ruts. It was after I started to poke around in the details of the individual lives of those on the Straight and Narrow Way that I realized how true Erikson's words were about the need to explore options as part of defining who you are and what you believe in. If you grab on to the first option that appears interesting to you and never challenge or question it, either because you're afraid to or because you are pressured not to, your commitments will not be as rewarding as they would have been had you allowed yourself to think about options (even if you remain with your original choice).

So, how often do you have to reevaluate your commitments? Every year? Every five years? Every ten? Well, those who view adulthood as a series of regular clocklike transitions would probably be able to come up with a number here, and my guess is that it would be every ten years. However, as I've already said, I think it's unrealistic to plot our paths through adulthood according to age-based goals. So I wouldn't whip out a set number for how often you should take stock and make a change just for the sake of it.

Ironically, some of my colleagues doing research on Erikson's theory of identity as it applies to adulthood would say that as long as you've gone through one period of exploration in your life, it is enough for you to be considered having "achieved" your identity (rather than being "foreclosed"). I always thought that was a pretty weak position, and in fact I had quite a few arguments on paper and in person with the researchers who had no problem classifying people in their forties on the basis of how they responded to questions about identity crises in their teens. It just didn't make sense to me. We need to evaluate people according to where they are now as well as where they have been.

Now that I've persuaded you not to expect any kind of simple answer, are you holding your breath, still waiting for me to utter the magic formula? How often *do* you have to evaluate your commitments to avoid middle-aged stagnation? Since I'm a psychologist, you might expect me to say, "How often do *you* think you have to evaluate your commitments?" In fact, my response is closer to this stereotypical psychobabble reply than I wish. I do think that when you face a possible choice point, such as when someone asks if you'd like to be considered for a new job, you should at least give it a second look. Maybe it's the worst idea you've ever heard, or maybe it scares you to think of doing something radical like picking up your possessions and plunking them down three thousand miles away, but at least investigate the possibility.

What about your close relationships? Should your spouse or partner get the careful appraisal every so often? I don't want to say yes to that in quite the same prescriptive way. I would never recommend to anyone that they switch partners just to avoid stability! Instead I would argue that you never actually want to take your close relationships for granted, because then over time I can guarantee that they will get stale.

Let's go back to looking at who you are now and what you might do to change. If, after taking the Pathways Test, you've diagnosed your pathway as Straight and Narrow, you are ready to take the next step, which is to begin to tweak your routine or at least think about tweaking it. Analyze the thinking that went into the choices that originally put you on your particular life path. If you are acting out a role picked for you by someone else (such as your parents), then on some level you might begin to wonder why you didn't take control of your own life earlier. But you needn't be frightened or threatened by this realization. Rather than waiting for everything to blow, like a clogged drain, you can release in slight and safe ways some of the pressure of unhappiness that has been building up. It can be something seemingly insignificant, like ditching that navy-blue blazer or letting your hair perm grow out. By seeing that you won't fall apart if you make these minor adjustments, you can then work your way up to something more adventurous that engages your mind and emotions on a deeper level.

These changes might include releasing yourself from activities in your daily routine that no longer give you joy. If you're a teacher who's taught the same course or classroom for twenty or thirty years, see if you can venture into a slightly different subject matter or age group. If your company has you pegged as the go-to person in a specific area, see if they can allow you to develop your skills in a slightly altered version of that specialty. You don't have to venture all that far away to stretch yourself, but you should try to venture somewhere. Change is built into the fabric of our being. As Freud stated in his book *Civilization and Its Discontents,* "We are so made that we can derive intense enjoyment only from a contrast and very little from a state of things." If we want to feel fulfilled, we need to find ways to shake up the state of things, if only just a bit.

CHAPTER 7

The Downward Slope

As a scientist, my job is to maintain an objective approach and to view participants in each of my studies in as detached a manner as possible. However, it is natural when peering into the lives and psyches of people you have investigated for decades to take a personal interest in what happens to them. You want them to do well and be happy, and when they don't do well you empathize with their disappointment and unhappiness.

Studying the people on the Meandering Way and the Straight and Narrow Way often caused me to wince when I saw not only their current unhappiness but the patterns they followed from college through the present that led them to feel unfulfilled. Watching the people on the Downward Slope pursue a series of poor decisions made me literally want to reach out and turn them 180 degrees away from where they were headed. I wanted so much to help them reverse the negative course that they seemed destined to pursue.

Whether you are unhappy because you shot yourself in the foot or because you were too risk-aversive or were unable to make up your mind, the result is the same. It might seem like academic nitpicking to decide which pathway is worse. However, there are advantages to distinguishing each of these unfulfilling pathways from one another. If you know you are on the Meandering Way, you can try to solidify your priorities as you strengthen your identity. For those on the Straight and Narrow Way, the antidote is to broaden your horizons and test alternatives. If you're a victim of the Downward Slope, knowledge about your pathway may help you cut your losses as you gain understanding about why you are preventing yourself from making more satisfying and fulfilling life decisions.

As I reflect on the people who are on the Downward Slope, I'm reminded of a conversation I had with a fellow clinical psychologist recently. We were discussing the common experience that psychologists have (or even students of psychology) when we meet people who ask us our occupation or field of study. The typical response we get is "Oh, so I suppose now you're going to analyze me." I always used to say, "No, of course not, that's just a myth about psychologists," or words to that effect to relieve their anxiety. However, one day I realized that no one believed me anyway, and besides, they weren't totally wrong. Psychologists do analyze behavior. It's what we're good at! So I've now started joking back with the retort, "Yes, I am going to analyze you, and the billing will start now."

Psychologists really can't help but analyze other people's behavior. To stop it would be tantamount to turning off our brains. The colleague I was talking with pointed out an intriguing twist. She tells people who ask if she's analyzing them that she's actually analyzing herself, not them. It's her reactions to others that tell her more about a person than her analysis of what they are saying or doing. That's a pretty Freudian response, and I might get some puzzled looks if I actually said that to total strangers. However, her comment isn't that far off from my own experience.

In conducting the research for this book, my personal reactions have become almost as much a part of the data as the facts that I have on file for each participant. For people on the Downward Slope, I was reacting in some cases to the ironic way in which their outward accomplishments were not mirrored by inner satisfaction. Ideally, the people who can be proud of what they've done with their lives should also have inward feelings of fulfillment. When this doesn't happen, it's frustrating and disappointing for anyone who believes that working hard and achieving your goals should be the keys to happiness. As you read these stories, you may find yourself having the same reaction. At the same time, perhaps like me you'll be thinking of ways to stop the damage these people are inflicting on themselves and turn their lives in a positive direction.

Frank

A major player in what at the time was the highly profitable mortgage loan sector, Frank should have been sitting on top of the world. All of the facts at my disposal indicated that he was a wealthy and powerful man: his prestigious occupation, his address in a swanky neighborhood. But we know that material success is not the key to happiness. I knew from his answers to my questions that he was dissatisfied with his life, cynical and distrustful, inhibited, uncertain of his identity, and despairing about his life's decisions. To understand the discrepancy between his outer success and his inner turmoil, I began to examine in depth the on-the-record revelations of his past business dealings.

But first of all, how did Frank get to be so despondent about his life? His early days seemed promising enough. In his late twenties, as a finance major getting a degree from a top program, he took a low-paying job in a community reinvestment corporation, where he could put his training to use in an important public-service role. As a financial advisor, he could invent the programs necessary to help develop housing and retail properties in the rundown urban areas of a Rust Belt city experiencing high unemployment and crime rates. His work directly benefited thousands of people. Perhaps reflecting his sense of commitment to working for the public good, Frank's identity scores showed a large jump between his college days and his early thirties. That would suggest that Frank had found himself and his purpose in life through this work.

There were some warning signs, though, even at that time, that all might not have a happy ending. His identity score at the age of thirty-one was actually the only one of the set showing favorable resolution of his personality issues. All the other scores were in the unfavorable direction. Something else was going on to depress his other personality scores, perhaps reflected in the fact that he was to divorce only a few years after that phase of testing was completed.

It's a chicken-and-egg dilemma: It's possible that Frank's low personality scores caused family strife, or it could be that his family strife caused his personality scores to dip. That he may have been suffering inner conflicts that contributed to the disintegration of his marriage is supported by the fact that although his scores bounced back somewhat by his fifties, they were never to go as high as they were in college. What might have contributed to this downward trend? He was moving up the rungs of the reinvestment company, reaching a high-level executive position. It would not make sense, then, that he would have been fired. But, in fact, he ended his employment in his midthirties to enter the growing private mortgage-lending industry, eventually to go straight to the top of a major corporation, where presumably his salary made a precipitous rise.

Now let's go back to those personality scores just prior to leaving his community-reinvestment position and his feelings of frustration in his early thirties. Was he unhappy with his career decision to enter that public-sector job? Did he find that the salary was so out of line with those of his classmates from graduate school that he felt like a fool for not getting into the private sector? Did his wife complain that his earnings were too low? Did he want a more lucrative lifestyle: a larger house, bigger car, more creature comforts? If so, his salary simply was not going to cut it for him. I have no way of knowing what the exact circumstances were, but I do know that before long he was on the other side of the fence, working in one of the companies that would ultimately be involved in taking advantage of the very people he had once worked so hard to protect.

I had to connect the dots from his early-thirties scores to those from his late fifties because he didn't complete the age-forty-two testing. In those twenty years, he did show slight improvements in everything except ego integrity (which plummeted). I then set about to try to imagine what was going on in Frank's life in between the two data points. I'd already figured out that he was earning a high salary and most likely living the lifestyle of a prestigious business executive in charge of major financial and even political decisions. In learning about that company, I found evidence of dealings that, if not shady, at least involved questionable ethics. I imagined that there might have been days if not months or years in which Frank was put in the position of having to defend his company's actions when they may not have had the best interests of the average citizen at heart.

Perhaps he was involved in activities such as the work of the agency he'd left, offering inflatable mortgages and untenable loans to people who would ultimately not be able to make payments once the interest shot up. Perhaps these types of activities plagued him with guilt about his decision to leave public service.

It's possible that when he originally accepted the mortgage-industry offer, he told himself that he could still help people even while working in the private sector. Lending institutions want to aid people in need of credit, and they need executives who are familiar with economic trends to help them help people. However, once in the position, some of the incentives and perks may have begun to crowd out Frank's well-intentioned interests. Lured into this trap, he may have felt that he was changing in ways that deviated further and further from the ambitions of his youth.

I will never know for sure, but perhaps it was because of the change in Frank's focus that his wife found it increasingly difficult to live with him. It might also be that the long hours and frequent trips that such a position would have required led to his wife's leaving him. Although Frank eventually remarried in his late forties, he had no children. Perhaps he didn't want a family, but judging from his generativity scores, I didn't see any evidence that this was the case. Without children, Frank's life lacked the fleshing out that children could have provided, a balance to his hectic and high-flying career.

Like so many of us who bring our youthful goals more in line with adult realities, Frank is not a bad man. He is not immoral or deceitful. He did not mean for his life to spin a bit out of control in this way, but somehow it just happened to him. Now he's fifty-five and wealthy, important, and well regarded in his profession. All would be well if only he didn't feel that twinge of despair, the belief that he has made mistakes that he cannot correct, and the regret over the accumulation of choices that created his life pathway.

What could we tell Frank to help him feel better about himself? He cannot, in fact, change the past, the years of being a mogul in the type of corporation that engaged in practices he at one time would have fought against. He cannot undo a life pathway that led him to material success but increasingly away from his youthful ambitions.

Perhaps the best advice we could give Frank is to help him focus on his accomplishments instead of his failures. For instance, it is true that Frank veered away from his initial intention to work in the public sector. However, in his current role, he has probably helped many thousands of people receive the financing that they need to start their own small businesses or own their first home. His company sponsors educational programs, scholarships, and an up-to-date website geared toward informing the public about financial management. It is true that his organization is not 100 percent good, but nor is it 100 percent bad. We could tell Frank to focus on these positive features of his work. Although many of us are inclined to dwell on our career failures, a bit of reorienting can help us take a more nuanced view of our job pathways and see where they have succeeded. And if you are young enough to change your pathway, then the task is that much easier—look ahead, see how you think you will feel about yourself in ten or twenty years, and make your adjustments now.

Change is always possible. Though he is in his midfifties, Frank isn't necessarily stuck. Why not look into a move to a nonprofit, or even back to a community agency? He is still at the top of his game and, compared with when he was younger, has a good deal of real-world experience. On the other hand, if he is truly convinced that it is too late to change jobs (or too much of a financial sacrifice), why not explore ways that he can work within the organization to improve services to consumers? Or start an internship program?

Let's now assume that Frank's malaise is not limited to his occupational pathway—probably a reasonable assumption. Like most everyone who gets married, Frank believed his relationship would last "till death do us part." And like nearly everyone who gets married in their early twenties, particularly in his generation, Frank would have been expected to have a family. His pathway did not take him toward either of these goals. If your pathway also took an unexpected turn in one or both of these areas, how do you feel about it? Are you ashamed? What about regret? In Frank's case, shame has turned to a strong and piercing sense of regret.

Certainly it would be wise for Frank to consider the possibility of changing what seems to him like an immutable relationship pathway. At any age, we can get involved in the lives of young people. Even though he didn't have his own children, he and his wife could adopt a child, or if they don't want to take such a radical step, they could find a way to serve as mentors, such as through the Big Brothers Big Sisters program. If these steps don't work, Frank can overcome his feelings of isolation and despair by actively reexamining the way he looks back on his life.

We can't simply erase the black marks from the scorecard of our past accomplishments. Instead do what the successful and happy people do when they think about their pasts—engage in a little beneficial self-deception. Most people have a pretty healthy sense of self-regard. As they get older, a bit more of this self-regard is increasingly needed as a buffer against the reality of their own shortcomings and disappointments. Older people who manage to feel good about themselves and their accomplishments do so by ever so slightly twisting or distorting the memories of the events in their lives so that they reflect favorably on their sense of identity.

If you find this to be an unpalatable solution, I recommend conducting a "life review." Invented by Robert N. Butler, a world-renowned psychiatrist (and former head of the National Institute on Aging and inventor of the term "ageism"), the life review can help you turn despair into ego integrity. Think about past events, including those that make you feel ashamed, and come to grips with them. Look at the forces that were impinging upon you at the time. Like Frank, perhaps you made decisions based on the temptation of a desirable position, or maybe your feelings about the person you picked as your life partner started to erode. Why did this happen, and what does it say about you?

As you ponder these questions, keep yourself focused on the fact that you cannot change the past, only the way you think about it. Some wounds heal more slowly than others, and of course some do not heal at all. However, those people who manage to cope successfully with the strains of comparing the life they have lived with the life they wish they had lived have learned to, as the song goes, "accentuate the positive." In Chapter 12, we'll talk more about the life review and how you can use it to your advantage.

Brian

Now I'm going to turn from a giant of the corporate marketplace to a participant who couldn't put together enough cash to pay his own rent and had to live in the home of a former girlfriend. Since he was not technically an outward success, Brian's life represents another variation of the Downward Slope. The path he took, however, could easily have been avoided. There were many ways in which he could have been a success at all levels.

A large number of people in my sample stayed with the study from college through their midfifties, and they form the primary focus of this book. Brian was one of a small group whom I had not heard from for more than three decades but who miraculously responded to the latest survey. When I first scored his personality test, I could see an uneven pattern of scores, but what really stood out was his exceptionally low ego integrity, qualifying him for a four-way tie for the seventh-lowest score on this scale out of everyone in the sample. This put him squarely in one of the unfulfilling pathways, but at first I wasn't sure which one.

As I dug deeper into Brian's personal history, I saw evidence of someone whose career seemed to bounce around from one unsuccessful venture to another. Though he called himself an account executive, priding himself on starting up a small ad agency, in reality his job titles were all in retail sales and he never stayed in one job for very long. Brian was using a post office box address with a zip code in Buffalo, New York, a city with which I was very familiar, and he seemed to be living in a fringe neighborhood between low-rent apartments and a university campus. I was intrigued by the fact that he didn't give a home address, which led me to believe that either he wanted to maintain his anonymity or he didn't have a permanent home. Brian was living with a woman with whom he'd once been romantically involved but who now definitely would be considered an ex. I wondered why he didn't just move out and live on his own, but then it struck me that he probably couldn't because of his lack of stable employment. Brian probably was forced into this less than ideal arrangement because he was just not able to make ends meet. Of course, people who are broke and living in unsatisfactory circumstances are still sometimes able to maintain their optimism and faith in humanity. What was the cause of Brian's low ego integrity scores?

When I decided to look at the website of his fledgling company, I found some information that gave me further insight into the answer to this question. Although he occasionally landed promising customers, none of them seemed to be currently employing his services. Some of his efforts seemed notable enough: He apparently had done work for several local nonprofits. His website, though flashy, had no substance; if you clicked on a link, you were led to a nonworking site or one that contained few details. Brian was forced to supplement his income with temporary retail jobs.

Although most of my sample participants picked up their industry scores considerably from their carefree college days, Brian never did. I didn't get the impression that he really had much of a commitment to any job, whether or not it was one that would bring him success in his main area of professional interest. The items on the industry scale that he endorsed were ones that asked whether he was a person who procrastinated, wasted his time, and didn't apply himself fully to his work. These qualities would certainly not be assets in the advertising industry. Given the competitiveness of that field, I had to conclude that Brian's lack of drive kept him from pushing himself hard enough to win coveted assignments.

But there was a second critical factor: Brian's cynicism. Somehow between his college days and his midfifties, Brian's sense of trust dipped from a reasonably normal level to one of the lowest in the sample. A combination of bitterness and dismay would have eroded his once idealistic interests and hopes for the future. He is deeply pessimistic, frustrated, and lacking in a basic sense of faith in himself. Combined with his low ego integrity scores, his profile is of a man who has a profound sense of personal failure. His inner turmoil is continually being reinforced by the lack of progress he has made in his career, a lack of progress contributed to by his own inability to stick to the basic requirements of his job.

The first step in restoring Brian's agony would be to address the cynicism that has spread through his personality. Why has he become so turned off from life? I would propose that over the years, a vicious cycle developed in which his loss of faith in himself triggered further declines in his enthusiasm toward work, leading to fewer contracts, and hence more bitterness.

Like Frank, Brian experienced conflicts in his feelings toward work that ricocheted into conflicts at home, adding another reason for him to question and doubt his life's accomplishments. In order to treat him, a therapist would need to help him stop this vicious cycle. It wouldn't happen all at once, but the process could be jump-started if he were given even a small platform of accomplishment to stand on and enjoy.

To get to that point, Brian would also have to address his problems in the area of industry. I know from studying the lives of other sample members that it's possible to increase your sense of industry. You do not have to be burdened for life by procrastination or a lack of work motivation. Sometimes people develop these poor work habits as an unconscious way to handicap themselves. Later I'll talk about survivor guilt—the inability of some people to enjoy being successful because to do so would threaten others close to them. Brian seems to be a victim of this tendency. He reminds me very much of an undergraduate student I once mentored who was constantly late with his assignments, who chronically underperformed, and who occasionally engaged in behaviors that put his status in the university in severe jeopardy. There was no intellectual reason for him not to succeed; his problems stemmed from an almost inexplicable desire to fail. So, for Brian to get off the Downward Slope, he would need to address the poor work attitudes that get in the way of his realizing his potential. It might take baby steps to get there, but if he were able to slow or even stop sabotaging his own efforts to succeed, he could start turning his life around.

Sandra

Our next sample member on the Downward Slope, Sandra, presents an intriguing contradiction that illustrates another facet of this pathway: anger and regret about achieving goals of youth too late in life to do much good.

Like Brian, whose trust and ego integrity scores were among the lowest in the sample, Sandra felt profound regret over her life's mistakes and wished she could rewrite her past. Unlike Brian, however, Sandra reached a fair measure of success by her midfifties. A full-time homemaker for many years, she is now a prominent state representative regarded by her party as a rising star. She described her job without much fanfare on her questionnaires, but it was only when I looked up her address that I was able to see just how much her political career had taken off. A champion of public school education, Sandra, I would have thought, could not have been more pleased with herself and what she was able to accomplish at this stage of her life. Yet she endorsed items on the questionnaires such as "Regret the mistakes I've made," "Think about my failures," and "Never get what I want."

Regrets her mistakes? Doesn't get what she wants? Are these the sentiments of a woman who has finally achieved what must have been a lifelong dream? Explanations for these responses come from answers to other items that she endorsed on the ego integrity scale: "Don't have enough time to do what I want to," "Would change my life if I could live it over." Therein lie some clues as to why Sandra is so miserable and why she qualifies for the Downward Slope. For some people, getting what you want but getting it "too late" can be worse than not getting it at all. As much as she was enjoying her success, it only made more poignant the fact that her political skills had gone unused for all that time. She'd have a few more years left in her, but she knew the real train had passed her by.

The irony of Sandra's situation is, of course, that she was doing exactly what she wanted to with her life, albeit about thirty years later than she probably considered ideal. Realizing such success at her age had probably led her to think that if she had started earlier, she would have been capable of achieving much, much more. The easy advice to Sandra might be: Your self-assessment is accurate. It is frustrating to think that you were stuck in the job of a homemaker for all those years and only now are expressing your true interests and talents. However, instead of thinking about your regrets, why not live in the moment? You can't get back those thirty years but you can enjoy the next five or ten.

Admittedly, that advice is probably too glib and wouldn't be terribly effective. To turn Sandra's viewpoint around, then, we would need to explore other approaches. My first thought when Sandra's success in state politics became apparent was that her many years as a homemaker may have contributed to, rather than detracted from, her eventual success as a campaigner. Years of attending parent-teacher organization meetings more than likely gave her ample material on which to base her platform. Spending time with the other parents, talking about issues ranging from school funding to curriculum, may have given her practice in refining and sharpening her debate skills. When she was in college, she had pretty high initiative scores, suggesting that she had a playful side, and perhaps it was that inventiveness and irreverence that provided the foundations for her later development as an engaging and effective campaigner who kept her audiences entertained as well as informed. Her ability to defeat her opponent, himself a popular local figure, suggested that she had not only political savvy, but also charisma.

How would we turn these thoughts into helpful suggestions to relieve Sandra's despair? Showing her the connections between her past experiences and her current success would possibly allow her to appreciate that she wouldn't be who she is now without first being who she was for all those prior years. Thanks to those years, she has gotten more interesting and better able to share her experiences with others in a way that truly benefits them. And quite honestly, she is not that old; she still has many years left in her career to run for higher office.

Other possibilities also come to mind for providing people like Sandra with a way out of the Downward Slope. We all know people who are unable to simply sit back and enjoy their success. After they accomplish one goal, they immediately focus on the next one. They constantly torture themselves with what they *could* have, and don't think about what they *do* have. Sandra could learn how to pat herself on the back for getting where she is, or she could do what the Erhard Seminars Training (EST) school of therapy calls "living in the moment."

We've all heard advice such as "count your blessings," but putting this advice into the context of my study, we can see that over time the self-berating that people on the Downward Slope engage in erodes their ability to develop the components of their personalities that will allow them to come to grips with why they are on this planet. Sandra's sense of despair was the result of a lifetime of small dissatisfactions that eventually wore down her ability to reap pleasure from what in fact was an impressive set of midlife accomplishments.

Lawrence

The essence of ego integrity is the feeling that you are connected with the world at large and are making it a better place. It would thus be logical to assume that one of the highest ego integrity scores would be Lawrence's. He has devoted his life to helping others meet both their spiritual and material needs by serving as a chaplain in a ministry devoted to working on behalf of impoverished people in developing countries. Lawrence has lived in some of the most desolate places on the planet, providing assistance in communities suffering from political injustice who are in need of education and basic services. He has achieved a fair degree of public prominence and respect for his humanitarian activities.

But of course, you wouldn't be reading about Lawrence in the Downward Slope chapter if his personality corresponded to this expectation of high ego integrity and life satisfaction. Unfortunately, Lawrence's notable accomplishments and career of dedication to others did not provide him with the comfort of knowing he has made a difference in the world.

College was a tough time for Lawrence, and about the only quality he did not lack in that era was his sense of identity, which was solid. Inhibited, pessimistic, and lonely, Lawrence was likely uncomfortable in most situations, particularly social ones. It is somewhat surprising, then, that he decided to begin his career by entering a theological seminary and becoming a pastor. Since he remained in this post for only four years after completing his master's degree, it would seem that he wasn't very satisfied with that choice.

Thus, his next career move didn't really make sense to me. Lawrence chose to work as an English teacher in a remote rural community far from his own hometown, both in distance and in mentality. Not only would he still be involved in many social situations, but now he would be doing so in a completely unfamiliar place, with people he didn't know, and in a small town where he would clearly stand out as a newcomer. It hardly seemed like the perfect match of person to job. Eventually, Lawrence left teaching altogether and returned to the ministry, this time joining a private international agency devoted to working with the poor and undernourished throughout the world.

This move seemed to work out better for him, and by his early forties, Lawrence was not doing too poorly—except in the two key areas of trust and ego integrity. Though still agreeing with items on the questionnaires reflecting pessimistic beliefs and harsh self-judgments, he had managed to crawl out of some of his other holes. Perhaps after his years of service to the needs of others, he had become more convinced of his own ability to be a competent worker. Throughout that point and into his fifties, his sense of industry consistently increased. Lawrence seemed to typify that pattern of "catching up" that I discussed in Chapter 2. He also improved in his ability to get close to others. By his mid-fifties, he'd finally gotten married and now had a ten-year-old daughter.

Apart from these positive signs, I still found myself perplexed by Lawrence's overall sense of despondency. Erikson's theory would have us believe that a lifetime devoted to self-sacrifice for a cause that was clearly a noble one would have enabled Lawrence to connect the positive impact he had on others' lives to feelings of inner contentment. Even if we set Erikson's theory aside for the moment, other psychologists who speak of fulfillment through selfless dedication, such as Abraham Maslow, would have predicted that Lawrence would have been able to avoid the kind of existential panic that he chronically experienced throughout his adult years.

I suppose one answer to this question would be that Lawrence was simply a malcontent. Even though he was able to secure a family life for himself and provide invaluable services to victims of social injustice, Lawrence just could never let down his hair enough to feel good about what he was accomplishing. I suspect he may have been suffering from chronic depression, a problem that would interfere with his ability to interpret his experiences in a favorable light. Unlike Sandra, who couldn't enjoy the success she had finally achieved after all those years, Lawrence had continuously performed well in his career and had done all the right things.

According to one view of personality, Lawrence's malaise would be attributed to a lifelong disposition that he can never overcome. I personally don't believe in the position that people spend their entire lives stuck with the personality traits they either inherited or developed in their early years. Some of my trait-theory colleagues, such as psychologists Paul T. Costa, Jr., and Robert R. McCrae, have written extensively about personality stability after age thirty and have provided data based on their own questionnaires that they claim backs up this position. However, their argument has its flaws.

Another of my colleagues, sociologist Monika Ardelt, astutely observed that when you stretch out the interval between testings to longer than a few years, there is actually a great deal more variability than Costa and McCrae report. Others have criticized the ways that trait theory defines personality. If you define personality as a set of stable dispositions, then it is no surprise that personality is shown to remain stable. Trait theory has a great deal of utility, but its view of development has serious flaws.

So, according to the trait theory approach, Lawrence would indeed be seen as a chronic neurotic who can never hope to achieve inner feelings of satisfaction. However, if that were true, he would show more problems than he does and he would not have experienced continued personality growth from his forties through his fifties. Something specific, then, seems to tear at Lawrence's faith in himself and the world at large.

People who get on the Downward Slope may do so because of

personal failings, but an alternative explanation, and one that might help explain Lawrence's problems, is that there is something about the world that they incorporate into their psyches. Through his ministry work, Lawrence witnessed a variety of dire situations ranging from severe hunger to poverty and all that goes with these deprivations. After spending his entire career exposed to these disheartening conditions, he may have simply found it too hard to reconcile the reality of what he saw with any kind of hope for the world's future.

We might wonder why Lawrence immersed himself in such misfortune. Perhaps he felt that as a child of privilege he needed to give back. Once he did so, the guilt may have been too overwhelming for him. I still recall the way I felt when I worked at the local state hospital to complete my psychology internship as part of my postdoctoral clinical training. There were days when I left the locked ward there clutching my keys (which was what I sometimes felt differentiated me from the patients), thinking how lucky I was to be able to go home and spend evenings playing with my kids or relaxing with my husband over a glass of wine. On the inside, what type of evenings would my patients have? Even with the best overnight nursing care, I could be certain it wasn't a comfortable or pleasant existence. Perhaps Lawrence felt this discomfort, and over the years it took a severe toll on his ability to feel satisfied with his life and his decisions. Maybe he wished he had remained a teacher, or maybe he wished he could have done more than he was already doing.

ACTION PLAN

Turning a Downward Slope into an Upward Slope

Although the label "Downward Slope" would seem to imply that this is a pathway doomed to complete failure, as we've seen, you can be headed on this trajectory even if you are a success in the material world. Being on the Downward Slope means that you are feeling pangs of unhappiness and dissatisfaction that have caused you to drift downward over the years because of poor decisions, an inability to learn from your past mistakes, or negative events in the outside world that have prevented you from realizing your dreams of youth.

If you're on the Downward Slope, you probably don't need someone to point this out to you, because you already know it. The people from my study who were on this pathway were viscerally miserable. They believed that they were failures, or they regretted that their achievements were too little or too late.

When I first started to examine the lives of the people on the Downward Slope, I was convinced that they could benefit from a simple reality check, where they would be guided to appreciate their strengths. Many of them were, in objective terms, highly successful people who were obviously extremely competent. If they had cognitive therapy to help them adjust their expectations, they would come around just fine. But I realized that their despair was so severe that simply telling them to focus on the positive wasn't going to do it for them.

Unfortunately, some people do seem to have a need to self-destruct. As I mentioned earlier when discussing Brian's case, they fit a pattern that psychologists call "survivor guilt." The term originated from the stories of people who were the sole survivors of their families from the Holocaust, survivors who could not overcome the feeling that they did not deserve to be alive.

In ordinary life, people can feel survivor guilt for many reasons other than literal survival. Their guilt comes from other sources, most notably their feeling that they should not be doing better than someone (usually from their families) who is less fortunate than they are. Particularly difficult to overcome is the knowledge that you are deriving benefits from advantages that your parents didn't have.

You may know people who enact decisions based on survivor guilt, and perhaps you have even felt this yourself from time to time. It applies to people who are on their way to success but then somehow do something to sabotage themselves and prevent themselves from realizing their potential.

I suppose I think of it as passive-aggressiveness directed at yourself rather than at someone else. It's sometimes as ridiculous as getting caught engaging in an activity that will result in severe reprimands. The employee who downloads porn on a shared computer and "forgets" to clear his search history gets fired for violating the norms of the organization. Now he can be "assured" that he not only loses the job he has but will have trouble getting another job. Who in their right mind is going to give him a good reference? Or how about the new office assistant who pilfers from the petty cash fund? She is bound to be found out, most likely sooner rather than later. This will most likely "guarantee" that she will be asked to resign. Any time we engage in this kind of senseless behavior—where we irritate someone who can help us, oversleep for an important interview, or flagrantly do something that gets us caught—we should consider the possibility that we are trying unconsciously to thwart our own success, because being successful means that someone else might feel bad in comparison. We all want to be successful, right? Well, maybe not. Sometimes it is very hard to hold on to the accomplishments that we crave.

To help stop the self-destructive tendency in people on the Downward Slope, we must allow them to feel that it is okay to succeed. They need to know that they will not be hurting anyone if they surpass others' accomplishments, and that they don't need to punish themselves internally if they find that they are happier than someone else in their family. Sometimes these people will engage in a little testing of the waters to find out if you will hold it against them if they do well. They may observe how you react when they are successful in their domain of expertise. Do you seem hurt by their success, or are you genuinely happy for them? Do you try to retaliate if they do better than you? If you seem to escape unscathed, they will be reassured that it is all right for them to go on the route they've begun and continue to make progress.

What if you are on the Downward Slope? How can you overcome your own inability to enjoy success?

Well, as we've discussed, the first step is to tell yourself that it is fine to be successful. Other people in your life will certainly be happy for you. Don't feel that you have to mess up to make them feel better. Second, you must really force yourself to believe that when you do something that hurts your chances for success, it also makes those who love you feel truly unhappy. Most parents really want their children to do better in life than they did. In fact, it reflects well on them as parents. If you do well, your friends look good, and if you do poorly, then they look like they backed the wrong horse.

Being able to avoid bad choices, to revel in your triumphs, and to integrate into your sense of self the unavoidable mistakes you make are all the keys to achieving ego integrity and hence self-fulfillment. You don't need to punish yourself eternally with poor life decisions; nor do you need to protect others by limiting your ability to flourish.

If you have made mistakes that have hampered your ability to experience fulfillment, there may still be time to recover from those mistakes. You don't have to remain trapped in an unrewarding pattern of life forever. Acknowledging your mistakes and then moving on can be the first step toward positive change.

CHAPTER 8

The Triumphant Trail

Early in the process of making sense out of my study's data, I thought that a logical way to understand why people's personality scores changed over time would be to group them based on their life experiences. It made sense that if people were victims of negative events, their scores would suffer, while if they were the beneficiaries of positive events, they would show favorable personality growth. I soon found out that things weren't that simple.

First, as you've seen in previous chapters, a number of people whose lives were stable showed precipitous drops in their personality scores. Then I looked through the data from people on the Downward Slope—successful, often, but miserable. To further complicate the picture, I next discovered that people who suffered severe personal losses did not necessarily show a decline in their personality scores. If anything, the opposite was the case. As much as I would have liked to make a direct connection between life changes and personality changes, it was clear from the get-go that my job would not be this simple.

It was in this context that I started to develop the notion of the Triumphant Trail to capture the essence of sample participants whose lives had been dealt a severe blow but who nevertheless managed to come through either no worse off or, in some cases, better off than everyone else. I began to search for the identifying commonalities in their personalities that would help the rest of us cope with the adversity that we all inevitably face in our lives.

Bev

Bev is one of the most impressive examples of those on the Triumphant Trail. Early in my quest of tracking down the people who hadn't completed the questionnaires right away, I located Bev's email address. It was very shortly after I wrote to her asking for her participation that she replied with a brief but friendly yes. Only a few days after that, she returned the completed questionnaires. It was within a couple of weeks of my decision to go in hot pursuit after the missing participants, and when I got back her questionnaires, I was pretty excited to see that my plan for expanding the sample was working.

Knowing how precious every piece of data was at this point, I eagerly opened Bev's packet and got going right away on scoring it. At first things were looking pretty good because her questionnaire scores were so favorable. I expected that she was one of the lucky ones who had managed to work out her psychosocial issues and come to positive terms with what was probably a pretty good life. Then I started to read her answers to the questions about her work and family events. Her job as a librarian was going well for her. She gave up her paid employment for many years to become a full-time homemaker but then hopped back into the work world pretty much where she had left off. So career was obviously not her main interest, and since her husband provided a secure income as a surgeon, it didn't seem as though the family was hurting for money.

Up to this point, I viewed Bev's life as fairly typical and certainly par for the course among the noncareer women of the sample. Then the bomb dropped: She had filled out information about her children, which revealed that her middle daughter died at the age of twenty-three. I must have stared at that page for five minutes, questions rushing through my mind. This was a woman with a really healthy personality profile. There were no clues suggesting anything was wrong. Even more surprising, her life satisfaction was at the highest possible rating, though she did add an explanation indicating that the loss of her daughter nevertheless loomed in her mind.

How could this be? Losing a child *and* feeling so positive about her life? Any parent can relate to the known research finding that the death of a child is the most stressful event possible. Were Bev's personality scores distortions or were they denials of a deep, underlying unhappiness?

Naturally, I wondered how her daughter had died, and whether it was due to an accident or an illness. However, the answer to this question remains a mystery.

Unable to fill in that part of the equation, I next tried to fill in the bigger blank of how Bev was able to make it through such a devastating ordeal and still have a well-functioning and intact personality. Few investigators are able to trace backward from an event like this to the earlier data on personality that might provide clues to understanding such resilience. With nearly forty years of prior tests in hand, though, I could do exactly that.

One clue to Bev's ability to cope with this loss came from her scores on trust, the underpinning of personality that Erikson said is formed early in life. Many years ago, when she was in college, Bev was among the highest in the sample on this quality, at least prior to the death of her daughter. Following the tragedy, it seemed that trust was the quality to suffer most. Clearly the event had stirred up negative emotions even though she was eventually able to evaluate her life in a positive fashion overall.

Bev's story gave me insights into understanding how early psychological resilience prepares us for later challenges. In fact, psychologists talk about resilience, or the "hardy personality," as the basis for successfully coping with life stress. By examining Bev's personality development over time, I could see that her firm foundation of optimism, her ability to roll with the punches, her faith in herself, and her feelings of contentment allowed her to weather the ultimate test of her psychological resources.

Psychologists are also beginning to endorse a branch of study called "positive psychology," which focuses on the human potential for growth. This field has shown the advantages of maintaining an optimistic stance toward life in terms of everything from health to wealth to longevity to occupational success. Occasionally I kid around with my students about the term "positive" psychology. Clinical psychologists would hardly be able to be employed if it weren't for "negative" psychology. I say, "What was wrong with negative psychology, anyway? It kept us going for a hundred years."

Still, I agree that, basically, positive psychology is a worthwhile perspective. Looking only at deficits and pathology causes psychologists to ignore the very real driving force that each of us has that allows us to cope with our daily challenges. Rather than saying that misery is the norm (as Freud once observed), this more upbeat philosophy says that the norm is happiness, not neuroticism. When someone is depressed or anxious, there is something wrong that needs to be fixed; it is not the natural state of things. From this standpoint, Bev's adaptation is not an anomaly. Though the challenge was a tremendous one, to be sure, the fact that she overcame it suggests that the human ability to adapt to adversity is wide-ranging indeed.

Leonard

Triumph over tragedy can involve personal losses—as was the case with Bev—or it may involve overcoming threats to your psychological equilibrium from severe outside stressors that affect many other people as well. A veteran of the Vietnam War, Leonard was subjected to the type of adversity that caused many of his peers to develop combat-related post-traumatic stress disorder (PTSD). Instead of emerging from the experience with his personality and life in tatters, though, Leonard showed continued increases in all of the psychosocial dimensions.

Researchers Richard Tedeschi and Lawrence Calhoun first identified, in 1995, a phenomenon they dubbed "post-traumatic growth." When it was first proposed, this concept defied the conventional wisdom that trauma can only destroy, and not build, a personality. Although surviving adversity is a defining feature of the Triumphant Trail, the ability to thrive in response to adversity is what distinguishes Leonard from the others on this pathway.

Veterans of the Iraq and Afghanistan wars are now being routinely screened for the psychological effects of combat exposure, in large part as a result of the findings from Leonard's generation that showed the wide-ranging impact of battle involvement. Our current vets are also more likely to survive head injuries than were soldiers of previous generations, which leads to an entirely different range of phenomena associated with traumatic brain injury.

The psychological effects of war became evident when some Vietnam War soldiers continued to suffer for decades from the telltale symptoms of PTSD, including flashbacks, nightmares, intrusions, and even denial of their days in battle. Of course, psychological battle scars can be traced back to at least as early as World War I, when the term "shell shock" was used. The difference is that the Vietnam-era soldiers were not only exposed to combat stress but were also faced with mixed reactions in their homeland upon their return from Southeast Asia. They were hardly greeted with the kind of sympathetic reception that helped their fathers and grandfathers recover from their war experiences. In light of many of his peers' suffering, how could Leonard have done so well after returning from battle? As I thought about his case, I was reminded of an intriguing bit of research I have always found instructive for students of adult development. The research was conducted on World War II vets and used a method similar to my own in design: the Harvard Grant Study conducted by psychiatrist George Vaillant and his colleagues.

Vaillant was able to evaluate the predictors of traumatic reactions to combat by reviewing the earlier college scores of his participants. Those who had the most negative outcomes after World War II had had the weakest psychosocial resources in college. Veterans who were better able to cope with combat exposure had inner strengths that had mediated the impact of combat and had allowed them to emerge with their psychological health intact. And in some cases, the veterans emerged stronger than they'd been before entering battle. In Tom Brokaw's *The Greatest Generation,* we learned about some of these stories, albeit anecdotally, as survivors recalled how much their personalities had deepened and matured through their war experiences.

Now let's look at the aspects of Leonard's experience that allowed him to emerge from combat in Southeast Asia psychologically intact and in better shape than before. In college, he certainly did not stand out as one of the best-adjusted young men, or even as one of the sample's most assiduous students. If anything, his industry and identity scores were rather low, and he wasn't even particularly high on basic trust. He was, instead, relatively high in the area of autonomy and independence, the ability to stand on your own two feet. Going along with this area of strength was his record of leadership as the president of the student government association when the university, like many others at the time, was starting to undergo the tumult of unrest.

Leonard's leadership in student affairs earned him a selection as a recipient of a meritorious achievement award by a national newspaper. His focus on student government may have become his single purpose in life, and perhaps as a consequence, he gave less attention to some other areas. That meant that by the time he graduated, he hadn't given much thought to his career. Out of patriotism, a desire to pursue adventure, or a desire for a way station between college and a career, Leonard enrolled in Officer Candidate School and entered the United States Marine Corps as a second lieutenant almost immediately after graduating from college.

In the marines, Leonard served with valor, earning a Distinguished Flying Cross, and while completing his tour of duty, he seemed to have settled on a career choice. Shortly after returning from the war, he completed graduate school at a prestigious Midwest university. Having by now accumulated a set of strong credentials, he had no trouble getting hired by a small office-machine manufacturing plant located in the Chicago suburbs. Within a few years, he had moved to an executive position at the national level, and shortly after that, he started his own company. In the two decades since he founded it, his company has grown to become a corporation of national prominence, with Leonard at the helm in the role of CEO.

With all this outward success, what was happening to Leonard psychologically? For one thing, he wasn't replying to my requests to complete questionnaires, a fact that I couldn't continue to hold against him, since he did finally participate in the survey when he was in his fifties. Over the thirty-four years between testings, his growth in all of the psychosocial dimensions was marked and significant. He was one of the people who, to use one of my initial data coding categories, "went up." (Very sophisticated, right?) Rather than being devastated by his combat experience in Vietnam, he seemed to have bounced back and grown psychologically healthier in every realm of functioning.

In the beginning of the book, I talked about how one life event can lead to another, to create a snowball effect over time. I don't think that Leonard's Vietnam experiences per se caused him to grow, but they certainly were a contributor to his development of self-confidence through crystallization of his identity. Already entering the theater of war with high levels of autonomy and a record of accomplishment in college, his ability to get along with people and his inner directedness probably served as great buffers between himself and the world of devastation and destruction going on around him.

Leonard's resilience contrasts sharply with the experience of Paul, who, you may recall from Chapter 1, is a man whose personality scores reached pathologically low levels across all dimensions, particularly in the area of ego integrity. His life has become the antithesis of Leonard's. Living in isolation, Paul has not been able to shake off the images of his combat duty. Looking back at Paul's earlier scores in college, we can see why this was the case. He started out in life with negative scores on all of the scales except autonomy, which was Leonard's strength as well (although Paul's score was lower). But in the context of all those negative scores, even a moderately high sense of autonomy was not enough to carry Paul through the trials of his years on the front lines.

Adding to Leonard's ability to withstand and even grow from his experiences in his early years was undoubtedly his stable relationship base. His college intimacy scores were not particularly high, certainly not as high as some of the other men in the sample, and so it seemed a little odd to me that he married almost as soon as he graduated. However, pointing to the cyclical way that events in our lives can influence our personality, and our personality can in turn influence our life experiences, I would hypothesize that even if Leonard hadn't been quite ready for marriage at the time, his relationship plus his decision to enter the war helped him mature.

In contrast, Paul's intimacy scores were low even in college. When he married six years after graduation, his intimacy scores became slightly higher, but by midlife they had plummeted back downward. His relationship with his wife was clearly a volatile one. They had multiple separations over the years until they finally divorced.

What do you do if you're more like Paul than Leonard? If you aren't able to overcome adversity without suffering ill effects, are you doomed to a miserable existence? After all, you can't go back and rebuild personality qualities such as trust that were not well established when you were an infant. You can rework old trust issues when you're older, but it's asking a lot to start from the ground up and rebuild completely, at least without major intervention.

But we can all learn from the inspiring stories of people like Leonard. If we didn't think we could, we wouldn't watch the seemingly endless stream of television newscasts that show people who overcome personal tragedies. We view these cases and try to pull out the pieces that we could use if those disasters were to befall us (or if they have already).

Here is what I believe you can learn from Leonard's story. First, he did make up for some of his personality weaknesses by putting himself in a situation that would test, stretch, and challenge him. Then, I would venture to guess, he did not dwell on the negative experiences he confronted in that situation. It's quite possible that his experiences were not objectively as negative as Paul's, but even if they were, Leonard must have found a way to compartmentalize them and not allow them to invade his daily consciousness.

Psychologists Richard Lazarus and Susan Folkman referred to such mental gymnastics as emotion-focused coping, and although it can come perilously close to denial—which is usually thought of as a bad thing—there can be healthy aspects to this process. Lazarus once wrote an influential article, revolutionary at the time, on the adaptive value of denial. That concept really stuck with me. Although psychoanalysts are often horrified by the suggestion that you don't have to work through the defense mechanisms that protect you from anxiety, it made sense to me that there would be times when protecting ourselves from the truth could be a blessing. Lazarus showed us that we can all benefit from this strategy, particularly when we can't change a situation but can change the way we think about it.

Once you have the confidence of seeing that you don't have to fall apart in the face of tragedy or severe stress, your coping resources start to build up, even if ever so slightly, and you are better able to handle the next challenge that comes your way. In this step-by-step fashion, you can then expand your true coping abilities and your internal strength.

George

The death of a spouse is one of the most stressful events that anyone can endure; psychologists place it near the pinnacle of all life experiences that test our coping abilities. The loss is particularly hard when it comes in an unexpected manner, or prematurely. This was the case for George, whose wife died prior to the third round of testing, when he was in his early forties and by then the father of two sons and a daughter. George's struggle and eventual success in coping with this test of his resilience form the core of his life story.

Our lives are not controlled experiments, and we can therefore never know how they would have evolved if a condition had been slightly varied. I can't say that George would have continued along a positive path even if he hadn't experienced these tests of his inner strength, but I can certainly explain what happened to him after the fact using the data I had in hand.

I would say George was almost hypermature as a college student— very solid, hardworking, and open in his dealings with others; all good indicators. If there was a weak area, it was a relatively low score on identity, a little surprising given his many other strengths in related areas. In fact, as soon as he finished college, George enrolled in a graduate program in health administration, a program that required a clear career focus, especially considering that most of the people who took this route tended to have had some kind of on-the-job experience and he had not. Early in his grad-school days, George married, the next indication of his blossoming maturity. He seemed to be well on his way to a secure adulthood.

Then the death of his wife, which occurred when so much was going well in his life, led George's personality scores to take a nosedive in several key areas. First was his sense of trust. It had been among the highest in the sample in college, but now it hovered around the midpoint, compared to the others in the group. That was not as precipitous, though, as his drop in initiative, the willingness and ability to experiment with ideas and feelings. Identity, never one of his strong points— despite his hypermaturity—went down even further.

In the ensuing decade, George was to experience a series of positive life moves—he remarried, began a steady progression up the rungs of the nonprofit company where he worked, and gained a reasonably impressive reputation as a writer and speaker. Paralleling these accomplishments, George was starting to reassemble himself psychologically. Still hurting in the important areas of trust and initiative, George was nonetheless showing impressive gains in industry. His focus on his career, both inward and outward, did not jeopardize his commitment to his family, and his intimacy and generativity scores were thus also moving in a healthy direction.

By his midfifties, many of the earlier losses had been reversed, and he was even gaining in his feelings of satisfaction and ego integrity. Though he wasn't at the highest point among sample members, he was in much better shape than most, and his trust scores had bounced back considerably. I found this interesting in view of the commonly held but erroneous notion relating to Erikson's theory—that we close the books on our earlier stages when we are young. The trust dimension seemed to be particularly sensitive to the vicissitudes of George's life. The fact that it increased in midlife reinforces my interpretation of Erikson's theory, that it's never too late for us to regain our feelings of faith in our environment, even if our adult experiences have included harsh blows. And because his trust had at one point been high, he didn't require a thorough reworking of his personality to get back on track.

There was one anomaly in George's latest profile, and it's one that I'm not sure I will completely understand until the next round of testing. That was in the area of initiative, where George had always had one of the highest scores in college. Although it started to pick up when he was in his forties, after the drop precipitated by his first wife's death, for some reason it came crashing down in his fifties.

I actually had to rescore his data a couple of times to make sure there was no error, and for a scary moment, I worried that perhaps all the study's data had been incorrectly coded and scored. At first it just didn't seem possible. Breathing a big sigh of relief, I saw that the scores were in fact correct and not in error. Several possible reasons for George's low initiative score came to mind. On the positive side, George saw himself as ambitious, dynamic, somewhat adventurous, and sexually aware. These positive attributes were almost completely balanced by his low endorsement of most of the negative items, including "I'm all talk and no action"—a sentiment to which he heartily, though sadly, agreed.

In trying to understand this answer, which was such a deviation from his other reasonably positive self-assessments, I decided to take a closer look at George's career achievements. He had risen nicely up the ranks and had seemed to be headed for a company presidency or even a position as a high-ranking executive officer. But then for no apparent reason, he completely switched gears and was now working as a private consultant. Having reached a relatively prestigious position, he was out of the nonprofit world entirely, except for occasionally providing free services to small agencies in need of help. Had he been overlooked for a promotion he wanted? Had the board of his organization decided that he was no longer able to contribute? At times, such boards can treat high-level administrators very harshly. Perhaps George's ego had suffered some of that harsh treatment and as a result he felt that he was, in fact, "all talk" and not enough "action." Maybe his critics accused him of being someone who promised but didn't do, and he had come to believe them.

But from a big-picture perspective, George's story fits the profile of resilience. He has overcome a tremendous loss that occurred early in his life and under difficult circumstances. There were a few scars that took a number of years to heal, and some new scars that were yet to form. George had been blown out of his stable and steady track in life by a completely unanticipated loss, and recovery didn't come all that quickly. Even after he did recover, he was not completely immune to another setback, one involving midlife career disappointment and disenchantment with the system to which he had devoted so much of his energy and passion.

The most striking lesson we can learn from George's story is that we can bounce back from what may seem at the time to be the depths of grief and sadness. To me, George is a model of adaptability, a man who seems to toughen up a bit more each time life throws him another challenge. I'm not sure if he is completely out of the woods, but based on the tenacity he has shown so far, I think he will be ready the next time his coping skills are put to the test.

Sally

Living through the death of one spouse early in adulthood is challenge enough to an individual's resilience. Sally, who suffered the loss of one partner through death but also had another marriage end due to her husband's infidelity, somehow managed not only to endure but to transcend both losses. As the nurse care manager of an urban medical facility, Sally had dedicated her professional life to helping the poor and homeless gain better access to services. Although her job tests her optimism and faith in her fellow human beings, Sally has a solid profile of psychosocial scores, one that has remained unwaveringly high throughout her adult life.

Her twenties were a rough time for Sally. She married right out of college but three years later discovered her husband's infidelity. For someone who had grown up in a small midwestern town where everyone knew everyone, the affair must have come as a complete shock and humiliation to both Sally and her family.

Although intimacy was not Sally's greatest psychosocial strength, her scores were high enough, suggesting that she wanted to move on in life and search once again for a close and committed relationship. Within eighteen months, Sally was cohabitating with a new partner, and a year later, they married. However, this relationship was also to have an unhappy ending: Her husband died after only two years of what seemed to have been a happy marriage. How could she remain positive and optimistic about her life after suffering such profound loss and disappointment?

We can see some answers to this emerge from her scores in college, which were consistently high across all dimensions. Sally had a solid foundation of trust and a good sense of autonomy, initiative, and identity, and in comparison with her peers, she was highly motivated to work. Since she chose the premed track, not typical for college women at the time, she was most likely a serious student. Perhaps certain courses resonated with her more than others, in light of the counseling career she would eventually pursue.

After graduation, her life started to unravel bit by bit. Sally's job as a childhood educator ended when the program terminated her position. Next she tried a stint as a technician in the local hospital's blood lab, but she soon lost interest and decided to try graduate school, this time in school counseling. As we've seen, in her personal life, one relationship went bust and the second had a tragic ending. However, somehow Sally managed to avoid traveling the Downward Slope. She remained optimistic and work-oriented. Perhaps reflecting her career uncertainty, her identity was low, but still in the positive direction. It bounced back and remained high in her forties and fifties. She doesn't at all provide a portrait of a woman who has been devastated by her rocky life history. To look at her psychological scores alone, you'd never guess that she's had a tumultuous past.

Did Sally's passion for helping others, so evident in her eventual career choice, help her maintain her focus throughout these difficult personal times? Was her early optimism and faith in herself enough to buffer her against the strain of her young adult years? I would suspect that there were dark days when she questioned her career choice as well as the sad outcomes of her romantic commitments. The combination of her solid early personality and her desire to transcend her personal troubles to help others seems to have provided the resilience to weather those storms and emerge in midlife with a strong sense of personal fulfillment. As we will see in the next chapter, these are the elements in navigating our lives that give us inner strength to approach even the most challenging of stresses.

ACTION PLAN

How to Make Sure You Can Triumph over Adversity

In many ways, I think most of us would agree that it would be wonderful if our lives contained no adversity at all. No sickness, no unemployment, no failed ventures, no misfortunes, no divorces or relationship problems, and none of our family members or friends becoming ill or dying. Of course, such an idealized life is impossible. The best we can hope for is that we will endure these stresses and carry on, perhaps not just for our own sakes but for the benefit of those who need us to be strong.

If you've been through some of these experiences and don't feel you've overcome them, how can you get on the Triumphant Trail? What are the common elements of the stories of Bev, Leonard, George, and Sally that we can use to help us find their pathway?

Earlier I talked about the value of denial as a protection against severe trauma. I think that, in part, all of the stories of my sample participants on the Triumphant Trail involve a certain amount of denial. None of them let despair overwhelm them, even though they could easily have done so. Though their daily lives would certainly have been filled with painful reminders of their losses, they never gave in to the temptation to give up and stop moving forward.

There is no one formula, however, to remedy everyone's pain. If I've learned anything from studying my sample, it's that they approached their life situations from the unique perspective of their prior personalities. A person with a solid foundation of trust was better able to withstand loss, perhaps because he or she could more readily return to the baseline of optimism and faith in the world. As Erikson pointed out, early resolutions of life issues set the stage for our ability to overcome later stresses. If you never had that solid foundation to your personality, though, are you fated to become devastated each time your coping resources are stretched to their limit? Luckily, the answer is no. Your task may be made more difficult and you may require help, but it is still within your ability to navigate crises.

Let's look back at the qualities that make up the Triumphant Trail that I explained in Chapter 3 in talking about the scale items. It is your perception as well as the reality of your inner strength that can help guide you through those very tough times. Once you perceive that you can cope, you actually can cope better.

Another way to get onto the Triumphant Trail is to use denial as a temporary stopgap measure that you later supplement with a slower, long-term healing process of coping. Protecting yourself from immediate pain allows you to move on. And later you will benefit and become even stronger if you open yourself up to the feelings associated with the loss. One of my participants stated on her website the following philosophy: "It is wise to move on from your losses rather than trying to recover what you've lost." She wasn't a psychologist, but she could have been one, as she had clearly hit upon a secret to excellent mental health. Over the decades, she'd increased in every psychosocial dimension, including those at the base of Erikson's set of critical life issues. Rather than being limited by some of her personality weaknesses, she was able to expand these key components of adaptation and health.

However, we don't have to completely remove the painful memories to overcome our life's challenges. Southampton University researcher Katherine Carnelly and associates found that some widows continue to have "conversations" with their deceased spouses on a monthly basis for as long as thirty-five years after the death occurs. Although conventional psychodynamic wisdom talks about "working through" a loss, the newer views of bereavement propose that it is not unhealthy, and in fact may be beneficial, to incorporate the lost partner, family member, or friend into your own psyche. That person made us a part of who we are now; to excise him or her from our memories is like cutting out a piece of our own self.

The same may be true for significantly negative life events that tax our coping skills. These events become a part of us as much as the people whom we love and are close to. When Lazarus began to investigate coping with stress, he found that his participants would often embrace challenges by relabeling the experiences as tests of faith. This was a sign that they could handle adversity, or it was a testament to their ability to see a silver lining in the ugliest circumstance. Our trials are as much a part of our identities as are our successes.

CHAPTER 9

The Authentic Road

Life often presents us with extreme challenges, and if our coping strategies are up to these challenges, we take the pathway of those on the Triumphant Trail. However, many of life's challenges take a less extreme form, and many are also self-initiated. The people along the Authentic Road have chosen to make changes to express their innermost selves. As inspired as I was by the people on the Triumphant Trail who have overcome extreme adversity, I found myself gaining respect for the gutsy (and good) decisions made by people along the Authentic Road, people who strove to realize their full potential.

I began to group my study participants into the Authentic Road pathway once I started to realize that there needed to be a way to characterize the people who remained continually open to new routes of self-fulfillment even though they didn't particularly "need" to change (as in response to a crisis or because they were miserable). Although Erikson didn't specifically account for this type of life pattern when he defined the stages of personality development, this path represented to me a continuation of the sort of self-scrutiny that Erikson did regard as fundamental to adolescent identity formation. As I've already discussed when talking about the dangers of the Straight and Narrow Way, the ability to examine critically the decisions you've made so far about what to do with your life is essential to healthy adaptation and ultimately to self-fulfillment. If we wish to express who we truly are, we need to remain open to the possibility of growth and change by trying something new. It might not suit us, and we can return to our old modes of existence, but even a slight alteration will allow us to feel even more energized and excited about our lives.

The ability to express our true selves is seen by many psychological theories as lying at the heart of favorable adaptation. Before the days of positive psychology, the humanistic theories of Abraham Maslow and Carl Rogers, which I discussed briefly in Chapter 3, served as the framework for understanding positive growth throughout life. But even before these notable psychologists, there were psychoanalysts such as Karen Horney and Alfred Adler, contemporaries of Freud and later Erikson, who talked about the need to discover your true self as the basis for a healthy personality.

A little focus on Karen Horney in particular is instructive here for understanding how I approached the Authentic Road. I must admit that I have always loved her theory, and not only because she rejected Freud's notion of penis envy! No, I became a fan of Horney's work when I read her 1937 book *The Neurotic Personality of Our Time* (one of the first self-help books ever written), in which she explores the struggle between our "real" selves and our "false" selves. She argued that we become neurotic when we let our false selves win out over our real selves, and we achieve true inner peace when we follow the beat of our true inner selves.

If Horney had diagnosed my participants before they'd gotten on the Authentic Road, when their scores were low and their lives were somewhat in shambles, she would have keyed right in on their real self–false self discrepancy as the cause of their misery. Looking back now at the people I placed into this category, which I could do only after their life changes played out, I can see the wisdom in Horney's insights into what makes us truly happy, or, to put it in her terms, "non-neurotic." She believed that true happiness involves tearing down the false self and allowing the real self to shine through. The false self is the one that tries to put on a proud face to the outside world to cover up our real feelings about who we are. According to Horney, it's better to express your real self—even if that involves admitting your weaknesses—than to continue to assert that you are someone you are not. The people in my sample who could finally shake off the pretenses and do what was closest to their hearts were the ones who ultimately became the most happy and fulfilled.

As should be evident from this discussion, making a life change isn't enough to put us on the Authentic Road. We've seen lots of people make life changes that landed them in serious difficulties, both from an objective standpoint of miserable family or work situations and from a subjective standpoint of the participant being demoralized and despondent. For changes to turn us toward the Authentic Road, they must be ones that lead to greater inner fulfillment. It might mean that we finally admit that we aren't interested in the occupation our parents wanted us to have and instead reclaim our true interests in what we've always wanted to do but were afraid would disappoint them. Jerome, the archeologist we met in Chapter 1, is an example of someone who found the Authentic Road by making just such a change.

Not everyone on the Authentic Road went through a life-changing transformation. Some of the examples you will read about in the next few pages were people who kept making minor adjustments in what was already a life headed in a positive direction. The key to their fulfillment was being able to adjust when the situation demanded it. Flexibility, as long as it doesn't involve huge pendulum shifts, is an important adaptive mechanism to keep us on the road to fulfillment. Like the self-correcting mechanisms we use when driving, turning the wheel a bit to the right and a bit to the left, the flexibility shown by some of those on the Authentic Road engaged these important adjustment skills.

Loretta

People with severely troubled lives do form the grist for the psychologist's mill, but people who are able to express their true selves and do that effectively just as helpfully show us that psychological health is not just a mythical concept. By now it should be clear that my role as a researcher has often morphed into the role of a cheerleader who roots for her participants' happiness. Now that any notion of being completely objectively distant from my sample members has been brushed aside, I can share with gusto the lives of the Authentic Road travelers. It was really fun to read about what the people on the Authentic Road had done with their lives, and it was certainly gratifying to see their lives play out according to a principle I have long cherished—that change is always possible, no matter what our age.

Loretta is a woman to whom I felt particularly close throughout the course of the study because she was so conscientious about responding to my requests for participation. But more important, I always felt that she was refreshingly different from the majority of my business-oriented and professional sample, and I enjoyed reading about her exploits. Loretta was a free spirit who worked as a legal secretary but participated actively in a community arts organization. Literally serving as "receptionist by day" and "tie-dye artist by night," she engaged in crafts from weaving to spinning, and occasionally she gave art lessons to local high school students. Throughout her adult years, Loretta seemed willing to experiment with various pathways toward self-growth, but never in a way that would qualify as a crisis—midlife or otherwise.

Loretta had a pretty favorable set of personality scores between the time when she was in college and when she was in her late fifties, but they were by no means completely static. The biggest jumps for her occurred in her twenties, but she continued to progress in the area of identity, feeling increasingly confident and secure in herself from survey to survey. In fact, Loretta was a woman I thought about when writing my textbooks covering other studies of personality growth in adult women conducted by my colleagues across the country. Abigail Stewart and Ravenna Helson, who followed a sample of women slightly older than my own participants from an exclusive women's college, concluded that midlife development for women often involves gains in self-esteem and identity. Loretta seemed to personify that pattern as she grew not only in identity, but also in initiative and industry. She was evolving into an increasingly self-aware, insightful, and interesting person.

In contrast to some of the wealthy internationally renowned "who's who" types in my sample, Loretta was definitely living a low-key existence, particularly with regard to her occupational pursuits. Although I was convinced that she had a highly artistic and creative flair, it wasn't evident in what she did for a living—a mainly clerical job that probably paid less than the current cost of tuition at the private university she had attended. I wondered whether her parents lamented that they were not getting much of a financial return on their investment.

Indeed, Loretta's one doubtful area in an otherwise psychologically robust profile was a less than optimal satisfaction with work. She also reported that she didn't have enough time. I imagine that the low work satisfaction score was due to the mindless nature of the job path she had decided to pursue. But what about the feeling that she didn't have enough time to do what she wanted to do? This is scored in a negative direction in the scale on ego integrity, signifying dissatisfaction with the available time a person has left to accomplish her goals. My guess regarding why she chose to agree with that item is that she was getting more and more involved with her avocation and less with her vocation. She probably would have liked to spend more time in the pursuits she enjoys. Perhaps she is even counting down the days until she is able to retire and make art her full-time activity. Other responses throughout the questionnaire led me to think that she is increasingly defining herself by her artwork, where she can express her creativity.

Having time to devote to her love of art also brought out another quality within Loretta's personality: feelings of inner peace. Clearly she is a very social person, or she wouldn't have managed to survive for so long with the others in her close-knit group. But there is a part of her that prefers to spend time by herself to develop her internal self-awareness. It made me think that Loretta is working on achieving what psychologist Carl Jung called "individuation," in which people in midlife attempt to achieve a balance between their opposing personality tendencies. It seems that she is trying to gain insight into her thoughts and feelings while still seeking to feel connected with causes and concerns outside her own narrow self-interest.

Thinking about her life as a whole, I wondered how Loretta would relate to her baby boomer classmates who had gotten on the yuppie bandwagon back in the early 1980s. I could just imagine her at the fortieth class reunion talking to someone like Bruce, one of our Straight and Narrow friends. In this scene, she's got long flowing curly gray hair and a flowery skirt, and Bruce is sporting his male uniform of khaki pants and a navy blazer. There's a good chance that he would not approve of her lifestyle. However, I also bet that he would be secretly envious of the freewheeling direction her life has taken. For her part, I guess that Loretta would be thanking her lucky stars that she managed to avoid (a) marrying someone like Bruce, and (b) becoming someone like Bruce. As my imaginary interchange unfolded, I hoped that something about that meeting leads Bruce to experiment and find his way to the Authentic Road and out of his midlife malaise.

Bart

Although I love my job, there are times when I think it would be just great to leave it all behind and pursue one of my other passions—knitting. For some reason, I truly enjoy converting a ball of soft, fuzzy mohair into an airy, lacy scarf or shawl. Usually I don't even care about wearing most of what I create—I just like making it. So when I read about Bart, who quit his job as a business manager for a public relations firm and became involved full-time in his hobby of organic farming, I must admit that I toyed a bit with the notion of what my life would be like if I pursued that part of me and became a full-time knitter. Of course, if I had done that, you wouldn't be reading this book, not to mention that I also would have given up a big piece of what I feel is my life's mission. Besides, what would I do with all those scarves?

Anyway, returning to Bart's story, his route from administrator to organic farmer was not without its stops and starts. His first marriage tragically ended when he was in his early thirties, after his wife moved out and left him with two small boys to raise on his own. In part, then, Bart belongs on the Triumphant Trail, but that was not the whole story for him. Amazingly enough, his personality scores didn't take much of a hit from that experience, perhaps because, like Bev, he had a solid, consistent base of favorable scores across all of the personality dimensions. Facing what would have certainly been a test of his optimism and faith in himself, Bart was able to muster his other resources and survive the abrupt end of what seemed to be a good marriage and happy family life. The one area to suffer was his career. At the time that his wife left him, he was pursuing a graduate degree, undoubtedly so that he could advance to a position with greater autonomy. With the responsibilities of work, raising his young sons, and continuing his education, the latter was the only discretionary activity, so it was the one to fall by the wayside.

For the next ten years or so, Bart was relegated to remain at a level of administrative jobs that probably did not suit what would later emerge as his entrepreneurial side. Moving around from one uninspiring position to another, his personality profile remained robust. However, I got the impression that his heart wasn't in his work. Then, in his late forties, through a series of gradual moves, he finally escaped to pursue his true passion. The decision to leave his secure well-paying job and venture off into the unknown territory of organic farming required a strong dose of initiative combined with a good heaping of industry. In fact, those were Bart's two highest scores when he completed the survey in his forties. My guess is that he was on the verge of making his move when the testing was completed, because he entered his new career shortly after the third set of questionnaires was sent back to me in his early forties. I probably caught him in the midst of this transition, excited about being on the verge of changing his life, and full of optimism about his decision. By the time his fifties rolled around, Bart was securely and comfortably ensconced in this new life, the success of which was clear from the numerous online articles that hailed both the quality of his product and the well-run organization of his company.

One of the intriguing features of Bart's life-changing decisions, from the standpoint of my research design, is that I could see what he was like both before and after his transformation. If I were interviewing Bart now and asking him what he was like before expressing his entrepreneurial side, he might say "Oh, I was so miserable in that administrative job that I just had to get out of it." Alternatively, perhaps he would try to convince me that he'd always been a go-getter, and it was only when the right moment came along that he was able to pursue that side of himself. Or he might have attributed the change to a midlife crisis. In actuality, Bart was in pretty good shape psychologically all along, and, like Loretta, his lifelong strengths throughout his personality probably gave him both the insight necessary to make a good decision and the tenacity to hold on through the inevitably tough times when success wasn't so certain.

Bart's life story gave me some of my most powerful insights into the nature of the Authentic Road. He was seeking that most desirable of vocational situations, what the late vocational psychologist John Holland calls "congruence." According to Holland, we each seek the ideal match or fit between our personalities and our environments. If there is a mismatch or a lack of congruence between the two, we will keep plugging away at attempts to make things right until something clicks into place. When that magic event occurs (like the wheels spinning around until they find the right home in the codex in *The Da Vinci Code*), we feel satisfied and motivated to work harder. If we can't make that happen, we hate our jobs or at best feel that we are just marking time until we can escape through retirement.

Holland's vocational development theory is now the most encompassing of all approaches to understanding job success. In fact, the U.S. government adopted his theory in the late 1990s and now categorizes all occupations according to the six categories he developed as part of this theory: Artistic, Enterprising, Realistic, Social, Conventional, and Investigative. (You can actually find these on the Department of Labor website in the "O★NET system" if you want to see where your own job falls.) Bart fulfilled his personality needs for Enterprising and Artistic work, with some Investigative thrown into the mix, because the vocation that he eventually chose encompasses all those qualities. After he found congruence in his work, both his satisfaction and his feelings of fulfillment virtually maxed out.

Whenever I teach about Holland's theory, I feel compelled to point out that not everyone can afford to realize their innermost vocational aspirations, and not everyone has the opportunity to do so. There is actually a pretty good chance that you have already encountered Holland's job-personality match notion, because many career counselors use the framework, from high school to adult continuing-education counseling. There is even a test that job changers can consult, called the Self-Directed Search. The frustration herein can be to find out what you are ideally suited for, only to learn that there are no jobs in that field, or that people like you are unlikely to be hired for that kind of work.

Case in point: When I'm not fantasizing that I work in a knitting store, I imagine that I've become a musical comedy actress. It's a good thing that I didn't set my career sights on that goal, because according to several members of my family—and by that I mean my daughters—I should not even be allowed to do karaoke.

The moral of the story is to find congruence in your job, take careful stock of your abilities, and identify the possible obstacles to the kind of success you dream about. We've seen what disasters can befall people who change their lives drastically without making a careful assessment of their chances for success. Bart was able to use his considerable degree of self-awareness, along with what was probably a small stockpile of savings, to realize the yearnings of his heart.

Arlene

While congruence is the key to understanding Bart's travels on the Authentic Road, Arlene's experience shows us another angle to getting on this pathway. In fact, for the women in the sample, congruence was not just a matter of getting their ducks lined up in a row and then making a move. Those who opted for full-time motherhood, even if just for a while, had to take a more circuitous route.

Arlene found her way to the Authentic Road after spending ten years raising her family. Unlike Sandra, who achieved her dreams of becoming a successful politician in her fifties only to resent having gotten there so late in life, Arlene was thriving at the time of the last survey. She was enjoying every minute of her life as an active professional, earning a decent income, and developing her creative side at the same time. Not a bad combination for a woman in her midfifties.

Looking at her college scores alone, no one would have predicted the successful outcomes Arlene achieved later in life. She was barely hanging in there during college, around the low end for each personality dimension. Things got even worse in her early thirties, when she seemed to be demoralized, cynical, fatigued, and uncertain of her direction in life. To understand how Arlene reached that low point of her life, we have to work our way backward to her twenties.

After graduating from college, Arlene spent a year traveling through Europe taking odd jobs and enrolling in a few courses at Cambridge University. It must have been an idyllic time in her life. Who wouldn't like spending their days and nights among the best and brightest of the world, punting on the Cam River? Wandering through the cobblestone streets, browsing through the bookstores? Sitting around in the pubs at night debating everything from ancient philosophies to the morality of the Vietnam War? I can hardly imagine a better place to allow your intellect and your ego to thrive. Not to mention the fact that being in England would have given her opportunities to enjoy travel throughout Western Europe, all the while exposing herself to a wide variety of cultural experiences. It would have provided the antidote to

Arlene's college-era uncertainty and listlessness, a perfect way to jump-start her young life.

What happened next might very well have been the result of the "How ya gonna keep 'em down on the farm after they've seen Paree" syndrome. Her European adventures would have left an impression in her mind that would have presented a stark contrast to the reality of having to settle down and earn some money. As it turned out, she was to work for only a few short years at a fairly mundane position in an advertising agency in New York City. This didn't seem to fit at all with her training or her previous intellectual exploits. My guess is that as a result, her job wasn't very ego-involving and she didn't progress very far up the career ladder in her five years at the agency.

However, living in the big city had certain advantages. While enjoying the life of a young single career woman, Arlene met the man who became her husband, a manager on the rise in one of the largest ad agencies in the city. You might think that this was a dream come true—receiving a master's degree from one of the most prestigious schools in the world, playing out the single girl role for a few years, and capping it off with a marriage that would give her a considerable degree of stability and security.

Although she kept working for a while after the wedding, Arlene quit her job and became a full-time mother after her daughter was born. By the time she was pregnant with her second child, two years later, my follow-up questionnaire arrived on her doorstep. Perhaps it was the stress of handling a toddler while pregnant, but whatever the cause, Arlene was not in good psychological shape. Her sense of intimacy was fine, and her identity had picked up from its low point in college, but otherwise it seemed as though she was headed toward the Downward Slope.

Arlene's subsequent development shows us that people can find their stride in their forties and that they don't have to pass through a midlife crisis to do so. After reaching what was undoubtedly the bottom of the emotional barrel in her early thirties, Arlene took action to step off the mommy track and reengage in the world of work, but not in the commercial field of advertising. Instead she explored another career path that would eventually lead her to a vocation that would be more congruent with her personality, interests, and experiences. She decided to train to become a licensed professional counselor, focusing on helping other former working women reclaim their lives and identities after years of full-time motherhood.

It probably began with conversations with some of the other mothers as they sat through Little League practice or made the rounds of taking the children to music lessons. These women shared a common history of having graduated from college in the late 1960s at the tail end of the sea change in attitudes toward working women. Some women in my sample had chosen to pursue professional careers, but Arlene and her friends had opted for the more traditional lifestyle. Arlene's bitter regret about having made that choice was now converting to a determination to find her way back toward the pursuit of her earlier life goals. After she made the decision to seek a career in counseling, Arlene enrolled in a part-time doctoral program at a local university. It took considerable courage for her to take this final step in her professional preparation, given that she was at least twenty years older than most of the other students and had a lot more on her plate than they did. Perhaps her strong maternal streak (her own children were now just slightly younger than her classmates) would have made her popular.

Based on my experience with older students such as Arlene and my own stint in a postdoc in my late thirties, I would also hypothesize that she made notable contributions to class discussions. Middle-aged learners tend to be much more challenging (in a good way) than their younger counterparts, and are in search of explanations rather than answers. So her experience in school would have been rewarding all around.

By the time Arlene sent me the last set of questionnaires, her identity was continuing to burgeon, to reach the highest point yet of her life. When I checked back on her through the Web a couple of years later, Arlene had completed her graduate program and was actively employed in her new career. At the same time, I could see from these online entries that her kids were doing well, and I had the feeling she was justifiably proud of them. I'm sure the feelings were mutual.

Arlene's life pattern, one that consistently "moved up" (in my sophisticated statistical jargon), is attainable by anyone who is willing to take some risks and not be bound by the usual constraints we place on ourselves by virtue of our age, gender, or life circumstances. When looking at her successful life pattern, I was reminded of another concept that I occasionally borrow from Donald Super's theory of vocational psychology, that of "recycling." It's kind of a terrible term because it sounds like we're talking about garbage rather than a person's highest aspirations, but it does suggest that we can go through more than one set of developmental stages in expressing ourselves through our career pursuits.

Vocational theorist Gary Gottfredson once talked about the "three boxes of life"—education, work, and retirement—and our need to break out of them, particularly with the changing population dynamics of the late twentieth century. Arlene went a couple of times through the first two boxes of education and work and as a result has guaranteed herself a way to continue to grow in what I expect will be an unbounded fashion at least through her retirement years.

Kenneth

Now we turn to someone who got on the Authentic Road in a straight (but not narrow) fashion. Kenneth was a medical school professor and administrator with outstanding academic credentials and a long history of public service to the profession and the community, and he clearly was one of the "stars" of my sample. After reading his online bio, I was ready to sign up for a course with him because his work seemed so interesting. Maybe in another life, if I were not a full-time knitter or a musical theater diva, I would have pursued a career in medicine or health care!

It was inspiring to see how much Kenneth had done to promote a number of socially relevant causes as well as to train others to follow in his footsteps. With an M.D. and master's in public health, his early adult accomplishments foretold what would eventually become a distinguished career in an important area of research on policy. After seeing his public record, I was eager to take a peek inside the private record of my questionnaires, and I was gratified to see that this time there was a perfect match between the external and the internal.

You're probably thinking, "Wow, that's great! End of story. He was a well-adjusted college student and now he's a well-adjusted adult. Is there a catch?" Unfortunately, there is, but it is not anything I can detect within Kenneth's personality. His positive scores in college only continued to grow more favorable over time, and by his fifties, he'd hit the ceiling on one of the scales (industry) and become more optimistic and energetic than ever. However, this was not the case for his sister, Kathleen.

As it turned out, being close in age and attending the same college, both Kenneth and Kathleen were in the study, and so I was in the unique position of being able to compare them in college and then some thirty years later.

Like Kenneth, Kathleen had an impressive career, though not one that would place her in that "star" category. She had maintained a decent if not remarkable set of full-time positions in the business world. Back in college, though, her profile of scores could not have been any more different than those of her brother. She had, across the board, almost the lowest of anyone in the sample. By her fifties, she'd gained in industry and identity, but that was about it. A very bleak profile, and not at all what I would have expected, given Kenneth's sunny disposition, strong sense of purpose, and concern for the welfare of others.

They now lived about thirty miles away from each other, one in Dallas and the other in Fort Worth. Throughout their careers, they tended to live short distances from each other, even as they and their spouses switched jobs. I tried to picture what their life together was like when they were young. First of all, how did they get along as children? Why did two such disparate souls then decide to maintain their connection throughout adulthood? For whatever reason, they had decided to stick together.

Comparing their scores in college, Kathleen and Kenneth were reasonably close in their levels of intimacy. But since the men in the sample tended to get lower scores than the women on this personality dimension, a close score in this case doesn't necessarily mean they were similar, since Kathleen was far below the norm for other college women. I suppose her cynicism balanced his optimism, and his stability was a counterpoint to her insecurity. Remaining so close to his sister obviously provided him with some rewarding experiences if for no other reason than to give him the satisfaction of watching her grow, perhaps as some type of personal "project" on his part.

Kenneth clearly had found a way to the Authentic Road and, more important, a way to remain on that path throughout his adult life. He was in very good psychological shape in college and he managed to maintain that advantage by making a series of what seemed to be decisions that would allow him to express his true self. He became involved in a number of important issues ranging from the education of future physicians to making health care available to the uninsured at a time when to do so was not necessarily in vogue. He truly practiced in the community what he preached in his hospital classroom.

More to the point, as I will discuss in the next chapter, Kenneth was not at all into self-aggrandizement, but instead into doing something that would benefit others in need of help. Although his professional activities brought him renown, they were activities that were intrinsically geared toward true public service. Helping others just seemed to come naturally to him, and it was a quality that continued to grow throughout his life.

How to Abandon Your False Self and Find Your Own Authentic Road

Now that we've seen examples of people on the Authentic Road, I would venture to guess that you would agree that being on this pathway is clearly the way to guarantee your fulfillment. I also would go further than that and predict that if you asked most people to tell you which pathway they are on, apart from those who are truly depressed or in a self-defeatist frame of mind, most would enthusiastically describe themselves as happy and fulfilled. We are generally biased to report that we are in better shape than an outsider would think we are. In fact, sociologists have long known that on the average, people tend to rate themselves as happier than the "average" person, leaving us to wonder: Who is this average person? Be aware, then, that if you're going to get onto the Authentic Road, you have to answer the questions posed to you in Chapter 3 very honestly. If you fall short, see what you can do to rectify the situation, for this is the pathway that truly leads to self-fulfillment.

The key to success for some of those on the Authentic Road lay in part in their solid early beginnings. We must give Erikson his due in showing us the importance of resolving the early psychosocial crises of life in order to achieve success later in life. All else being equal, you're better off if you get a good start in life. But we can also see from the experiences of my participants that if you didn't have that advantage, you can still fulfill your inner potential.

Think about, for example, the issues of autonomy, one of Erikson's earliest stages. If you were self-doubting and unsure in your youth and even young adulthood, what can you do to change that now? For one thing, you can look back on the times when you have stood up for yourself and done what you wanted to or what you thought was right, and realize that if it was possible to do so then, you can do it again. Or if you've never been that bold, take one small step in that direction and allow yourself to experience the satisfaction of doing what you think is truly right rather than what you think you "should" do.

A second way you can rework some of the earlier personality issues in order to pave the way to greater self-expression is to develop your flexibility. One key quality of those on the Authentic Road is the ability to value a little experimentation over the comfort of stability, that old notion of "initiative" in Erikson's terms. As we've already seen, researchers investigating Erikson's theory in early adulthood pointed out the value of exploring alternatives rather than foreclosing on one choice. You will be more fulfilled if you can maintain an open mind and question your current commitments and even some of your most dearly held beliefs.

We can't keep making 180-degree turns every month, or even every six months, just to try this and that (or we would be Meanderers), but we can at least examine the attractiveness of those turns. When we engage in this self-scrutiny, we may end up exactly where we started, but it will be with a fuller appreciation that we are doing what we want to with our lives rather than settling for what we've fallen into doing out of habit or repetition.

We have now come, as it were, to the end of the pathways. These varied routes through adult life have ranged from the lows of frustration and despondency to the highs of self-expression and successful adaptation in response to even the worst of life's circumstances. In the next few chapters, we'll put together the main themes that underlie progress through each of these pathways and show how, regardless of the pathway you're on, it's never too late to take action so that you can realize your true identity. When you do so, as you'll soon learn, you will feel inwardly fulfilled and you will be making a lasting impression on the world that can be the true realization of your inner potential.

CHAPTER 10

Reflections on Adult Growth

If you took the diagnostic test in Chapter 3, you had an idea of which pathway you were on before you read about them in greater detail. But now it's time for another round of taking stock. Perhaps you've identified with one or another of my sample participants because their lives sounded somewhat like yours.

As you read about the people in my study, I hope you gained a sense of what it takes to jump from a negative to a positive pathway. Just as important, perhaps you have learned what helps people stay on positive pathways once they've found their way to them. I hope I've managed to convince you that you don't have to be stuck on a pathway that is taking you in a direction other than the one that you most desire. At the same time, if you're happy with the way your life is now, it's still important to evaluate continually how it's going. Lest you get complacent or inflexible, you should do an internal audit every now and then.

I certainly hope I've encouraged you to dispense with putting your life into neat little age-based intervals. Some historians have a tendency to think of the life of a nation as occurring in decades, for example, and to do so is equally problematic from the standpoint of understanding how historical events actually unfold. As tempting as it is, you can't put a naturally occurring phenomenon such as the life of a person or a country into discrete units.

In the field of adult development, the most famously wrongheaded attempt to segment our lives into distinct entities is the proposition that adulthood is punctuated at its midpoint by a full-blown crisis. I've touched now and then on the topic throughout the book, but now that you've seen the data showing the disparate lives of my participants, I'd like to confront comprehensively this issue once and for all.

The Myth of the Midlife Crisis

You know the plotline by heart: A man turns forty-five or so, ditches his wife for a twenty-five-year-old bartender, tells his boss he's through with the daily grind, starts donning a leather jacket, and buys a cherry-red sports car—or if he's really feeling midlife crisis-y, he buys a Harley. But psychological researchers, despite their best efforts, haven't been able to show that more than a fraction of the population experience something resembling a crisis in midlife, and even then, the definition of "crisis" and "midlife" are highly open to interpretation.

As you've seen by now from reading about the pathways, there is no one single route through the adult years. Still, it's worthwhile to take a look at where the concept of the midlife crisis came from and why it is so flawed.

The midlife crisis notion first began to creep into psychology late in the 1960s when the forty-six-year-old Yale professor and psychologist Daniel Levinson decided to examine his experiences of midlife malaise. He set out to investigate whether his own discontent and disillusionment with life was routine among all men between the ages of thirty-five and forty-five. Rounding up a few of his friends and colleagues, he organized a seminar on adult development. The men in the seminar, ranging through the forties, used the opportunity to discuss their previously unconscious fantasies and anxieties about aging.

Levinson soon felt that there was something universal about their revelations, and so he expanded his focus group beyond friends and colleagues. He found more men to interview, seeking to uncover if they too had troubling feelings regarding their middle years. By the time he finished his forty interviews, he had expanded his study to include not just the midlife crisis, but the period of adulthood spanning the early twenties to the midfifties, seeking to find regular patterns of change according to age. Ultimately, he concluded that these patterns of change occurred over approximately five- to seven-year periods.

Each stage represented a shifting of priorities and behaviors in what Levinson called the "life structure," the particular organization of the man's life at that point in time. The midlife transition was one of three major transition periods, including the transition to young adulthood in the early twenties and the transition to later adulthood in the early fifties. I will return to the concept of the life structure later, because of all Levinson's ideas, I think it's the one that has the most instructive value for helping us understand our own development.

Coincidentally, while Levinson was involved in his work at Yale, a psychiatrist at UCLA named Roger Gould also found himself personally driven to study the midlife period. Having reached his early forties, Gould was also feeling angst and confusion. In a process eerily similar to Levinson's self-exploration, Gould came to the conclusion upon his study's completion that he had gone through the same midlife crisis as the people in his study.

Like Levinson, Gould sought to identify regular patterns of personality change that would correspond to exact age periods of six- to seven-year intervals. According to Gould, if you were thirty-one, you were in the "Opening Up to What's Inside" stage, in which you started to listen to your inner needs and feelings. If you were fifty-two, you were in the "Beyond Mid-Life" stage, in which you realized that you alone were the one who directed the course of your life. The various stages in between involved a series of ups and downs, with the major down coinciding with the midlife crisis in the early forties. Gould tested his ideas on a sample of more than five hundred adults, and, unlike

Levinson, he included women in his original investigation. Rather than interview them, Gould developed a questionnaire culled from his clinical observations that asked people to indicate their agreement with a series of statements about their lives.

This idea of the midlife crisis gained a place in the popular culture through a popular work. Journalist Gail Sheehy had met with both Levinson and Gould to interview them for a magazine article. The article was very successful, and while the researchers were still working on their books, Sheehy wrote her own: *Passages: Predictable Crises of Adult Life*.

Sheehy's work struck a chord with the large and increasingly receptive audience of midlife adults, which gained the book instant recognition. The "passages" mentioned in the title referred to age-based stages in which psychological changes were associated with the passing of the decades. Clever labels such as the "trying 20s," the "catch 30s," and the "forlorn 40s" made the model even more appealing to the mass market. You could say that Sheehy was attempting to write *Dr. Spock's Baby and Child Care* for adults, many of whom had been raised in the era of Dr. Spock's advice for parents and felt comfortable with this type of guidance.

Shortly after Sheehy's book was published, Levinson rose to the occasion by publishing his own work, relying on another calendar metaphor for the title: *The Seasons of a Man's Life*. On the heels of Levinson's book came Gould's: *Transformations: Growth and Change in Adult Life*. Levinson and Gould, despite the modest success of their books, felt that they had been exploited by Sheehy, whose mass-produced paperback version emerged by far the most popular of the three titles. Gould sued Sheehy and eventually the case was settled, with Gould reportedly receiving $10,000 and 10 percent of the royalties from *Passages*. However, with more than five million books sold worldwide, Sheehy cashed in on her book royalties, and continues to do so today.

Remarkably, with all the finger-pointing about who was stealing what research from whom, the term "midlife crisis" was not original to any of the three authors. The actual phrase was picked up from the article "Death and the Midlife Crisis" published in 1965 by Elliott Jaques, a

Canadian psychiatrist. In this piece, published in an obscure psychoanalytic journal, Jaques examined the lives of famous people to provide evidence for the universal experience of anguish that occurs as we come to grips with our own mortality.

With the publication of the works by Levinson, Gould, and Sheehy, the gauntlet was thrown down for academic researchers working in the psychology of aging to examine objectively the ideas the myth perpetrators had so passionately put forward. Suspicion lurked in our minds because of our inherent skepticism about claims made that age "causes" personality changes. A basic tenet of our work, as you've learned already, is that development is a complex interaction of biology, psychology, and social context. We don't give any special value to chronological age as a causal factor in development. Besides, the evidence they presented didn't seem to fit with any of the data we ourselves had collected.

One of the first critics to argue that the midlife crisis idea was scientifically invalid was George Vaillant, a former Harvard professor and psychiatrist whom I referred to earlier as the lead investigator in a longitudinal study known as the Harvard Grant Study, which followed college men throughout their lives. In his own book, *Adaptation to Life,* published around the time of the midlife crisis craze, he took an entirely different approach to understanding the lives of his middle-aged male sample.

Vaillant's data showed that midlife is not divided into age-based stages. Rather, successful development depends on one's ability to react adaptively to stress encountered over one's lifetime. In that work, he defined what would later become a fundamental concept in modern psychiatry, that defense mechanisms can range in their degree of maturity. The mature defense mechanisms include such tactics as humor or intellectualization, in which we use our cognitive processes to handle anxiety. An example of immature defense mechanism is acting out, in which we act destructively or rashly. Often such actions—such as punching a hole in a wall in your house, which will only require a costly repair later—are against our own best interests. Vaillant first identified an overall pattern showing that people increasingly use mature defense mechanisms as they get older, a pattern since verified in numerous empirical studies by other researchers.

Among Vaillant's many fascinating observations were the comments he made concerning the association between crisis points in adulthood and age. Not denying that people can and do experience transition points, he dismissed the notion that age was the cause. "Certainly there is nothing magical about a given year," he wrote. In Vaillant's ongoing work on the project, now in collaboration with psychiatrist Robert Waldinger at Beth Israel Deaconess in Boston, numerous investigations have linked important personality changes to life events and social context, and with each publication, this idea continues to be reinforced.

I conducted my own in-depth investigation of identity development in midlife, in collaboration with sociologist Dale Dannefer. We identified a sample of almost one hundred adults ranging from twenty-one to sixty years old, selected to be representative of the general population in age, gender, and social class. The participants we chose were given in-depth interviews about the major areas in their lives that served to define their sense of self. The interviews focused on family, work, gender role, and values, but we also included a series of questions asking them to give us their views about how they had changed with age.

We also asked them whether age was an important part of their own identities and if they could identify any turning points in their lives. Dannefer developed a detailed life history interview in which he asked our participants what happened to them on a year-by-year basis. If a midlife crisis were going to emerge, it would surely have become evident in answers to these questions, but it never did. Our participants identified a variety of important events in their lives, but neither consciously nor subconsciously were these events linked to age.

At about the same time that the interview study was going on, my colleagues Paul T. Costa, Jr., and Robert R. McCrae, working on a large-scale study of veterans in Boston called the Normative Aging Study (which is ongoing), approached the problem from a different perspective. They already had a large amount of data attesting to the stability of the personality trait known as "neuroticism," which refers to a high degree of worry and anxiety, low self-esteem, and chronic self-doubting. If a midlife crisis were going to be evident, it would show up as a precipitous increase in this trait. The fact that this trait didn't change in the participants' forties was one piece of important data. Then the researchers went further and decided to devise a "midlife crisis scale" directly based on the writings of Levinson and Gould, with items intended to tap different facets of the experience. They gave the questionnaire to more than two hundred men ranging from thirty-five to seventy-nine years of age. Despite their best efforts, they found no age differences on the midlife crisis scale.

Finally, Costa and McCrae took advantage of the longitudinal nature of the Normative Aging Study and gave the participants the midlife crisis scale. Some of the participants in their forties did have elevated scores on this measure. As it turned out, these were the men whose neuroticism scores had also been higher back when they were in their thirties. So, perhaps people who suffer an apparent "midlife crisis" are not having a crisis specific to midlife. Perhaps these are the people who tend to be poorly adjusted throughout their lives, not just in their early forties. In other words, they would be just as likely to experience midlife crisis symptoms at age twenty and age sixty as they are to experience them at forty years of age.

You might think that adult development researchers would have stopped there, case closed. But there was one more empirical investigation yet to come. In some ways this was the most impressive. Cornell sociologist Elaine Wethington took the lead in heading up a paper based on the Midlife in the United States Study (MIDUS) begun in the mid-1990s, in which a national probability sample of adults ranging in age from their thirties to their sixties were asked, point-blank, whether they had experienced a midlife crisis, and if so, when. The results really slammed the door shut on the midlife crisis as a scientifically valid concept.

In Wethington's study, roughly one quarter of the sample agreed with the statement that they had experienced a midlife crisis. Not a negligible percentage, but far from the majority. However, what was most telling about the finding was the looseness of the concept of "midlife crisis." Participants who said they'd had a midlife crisis were using the term to apply to anything of a negative nature that had happened to them at some point in their adult years. By now the concept has become so widely accepted in the vernacular of everyday life that people use it to apply to everything from an encounter with feelings of mortality (the original definition) to dissatisfaction with their children's achievements or, more generally, to "stress."

Why, then, with no evidence to support it and plenty to dismiss it, won't the midlife crisis die? Having thought over this question for many years, I've come to see that the concept's popularity says something about what people want, if not what they experience. The midlife crisis plays into our fantasies that we never really have to grow up. We can keep making changes, looking for a way to express our inner selves, no matter how old we are. It is a theme that makes for good books, entertaining movies, and great daydreams.

Thinking about what might be different at midlife is a great way to escape from life's humdrum realities. Like the artist Paul Gauguin, who in his forties left his job as a Paris stockbroker to become an artist in Tahiti, we would all like to think it's at least possible to light out on a journey of self-discovery.

Another reason the midlife crisis stays put as a cultural icon is that people are just bad statisticians. Psychologists Amos Tversky and Daniel Kahneman call this the "availability heuristic," meaning that we tend to remember better an event that is vivid and compelling. Only the unusual stories stand out in our memories.

The availability heuristic explains very well indeed the perpetuation of the midlife crisis myth. You hear the story of a friend's husband who showed the "classic" signs of a midlife crisis. He dramatically quit his job, got a hair transplant, left his family, married a twenty-five-year-old woman, and (of course) got a flashy convertible. Your friends gossip about the big scandal and you remember his story more strongly than the lives of hundreds if not thousands of people you know who never even dye their hair or trade in their minivan for that trademark sports car. If you were to keep count, the score would be "midlife crisis: one; no midlife crisis: one thousand" (or however many people you know in their forties). But none of us actually keeps count. It's just the unusual stories that stand out in our memories.

All of this is fine in a way, but the myth can have a dark side. If we regard a person's unhappiness as a time-limited expression of midlife angst, we may not pay attention to the underlying problems that could be provoking disturbing feelings and behaviors. There is a misleading reductionism involved in attributing changes in midlife to a predictable crisis. By watering down a complex search for personal meaning to the banal playing out of a preordained scenario, we trivialize the experience. "Oh, he's just going through a midlife crisis," we say, whether referring to his purchase of a vacation condo in Belize or his giving up a familiar world and stepping out into the unknown to pursue a life's dream. In addition to being inaccurate, it's patronizing to interpret a person's attempt to venture off in an honest new direction in life as a second adolescence.

When we redefine the experience of a midlife changer as part of a predictable sequence of crises, we also distance and protect ourselves from the experience. Perhaps we are threatened by the fact that someone is taking a risk rather than settling for the status quo. After all, if someone else can do it, why can't we? Why haven't we? It's easier to see a person's search for self-fulfillment as the enactment of a foolish desire to return to one's youth than to see this search as a courageous desire to find a better life.

The irony is that there is nothing wrong with sticking with the status quo. We worked hard to get there. Our jobs aren't bad, we love our family, we like where we live, and we feel comfortable in our community, where we know many people and have some good friends. The problem occurs when we feel that we should change just to fit a mold. Still driving the white Camry? Still with our spouses—after all this time?

Still with the company—and don't want to branch out in new directions? What's wrong with you? In some ways, we've come to feel guilty if we don't seek a new pathway in midlife.

Of course, I do believe—and the data supports the claim—that it's always good to be open to change. The trick is not to feel pressured to change or to make changes that end up having disastrous consequences. Finding the pathway that best expresses our true selves is a process that can continue throughout life and needn't be locked into a particular decade.

The Power of Change

Although the midlife crisis notion fails to make the grade as a scientific concept, its popularity taps into the desire that all of us have to find the ideal balance between change and stability in our lives. In addition, Levinson's notion of the life structure conveys the idea that we are constantly building and remodeling the bits and pieces of our psyches, much as we shape and reshape our homes.

In my study, a consistent theme throughout the pathways is an underlying current of change and growth alternating with the desire for stability. It might be too strong a statement to say that to remain static is to wither away, but I don't think it's far from the truth. Life is about shifting the balance in favor of change, and try as we might to hold on forever to the best of moments, it's simply impossible.

The pathways that were the most successful in terms of making people feel vital and self-fulfilled were those that involved not only change but change that was adaptive. Change for the sake of change can sometimes bring grief, as we saw with the people on the Meandering Way and the Downward Slope. Failure to respond to changing life conditions, as in the Straight and Narrow Way, leads to people trying to hold on to what they have without accommodating the changing life circumstances with which they are confronted. For people on the Triumphant Trail, the changes certainly are not ones that are sought after or desired, but the ability to bend without breaking in response to these changes stems from a fundamental internal flexibility. On the Authentic Road, people's adaptations typically occur in a steadier manner throughout life, although in some cases, they wait a few years or even decades until they finally find their way to it.

As I analyzed the pathways, flexibility toward change certainly emerged as a central theme. Incorporated in the notion of change is the ability to make sacrifices. There is personal risk involved in leaving your comfort zone and stretching yourself to see how far you can go. The desire to do this can stem from a commitment to a purpose higher than simply generating tangible rewards for oneself. In my study, this quality was represented by a combination of generativity and ego integrity. People who do take risks and put themselves on the line are often motivated by a connection to a cause outside the self. Although Erikson's theory doesn't deal with "spirituality" per se, the people who scored high on generativity and ego integrity, despite some of the odds that they faced, would undoubtedly agree that they were not simply fighting their own personal battles in order to be successful or get recognition for their efforts.

Midlife Issues: Health, Work, and Family

An issue that assumes critical importance in midlife (if not earlier) is that of physical health. In the field of behavioral medicine, a concept that trumps all others in terms of predicting chronic disease, particularly heart disease, is the type A behavior pattern, or "type A personality," as it's often called. People who are hard-driving, competitive, pressured for time, impatient, and hostile toward others show an increased risk of hypertension and heart disease in their middle and later years.

Hostility can also pose a risk factor for the development of depression. In one study of University of North Carolina alumni led by Ilene Siegler of Duke University, people who were high on hostility in college were in midlife at higher risk for depression as well as a host of other deleterious changes in health and social functioning. If we relate this finding to the pathway notion, it would suggest that people on the Downward Slope can face significant health risks as their lives unfold while depression and anger continue to spiral.

For those on the Straight and Narrow Way, assuming they are not dealing with suppressed emotions such as resentment toward those people or conditions that keep them from changing, there may actually be some health benefits. The personality trait of conscientiousness, one that quite likely is high in these individuals, is related to better health in adulthood. In fact, the leading researcher of the type A personality, Meyer Friedman, found back in 1995 that people who were lower in conscientiousness in childhood were more likely to die at younger ages compared with people high in conscientiousness.

Later research confirmed this result and suggested that it's the control over their body weight that leads the people high in conscientiousness to live longer. The health benefits of conscientiousness continue well into late life. Costa and his colleagues studied more than one thousand Medicare recipients over a three- to five-year interval and found that self-discipline, one aspect of conscientiousness, predicted lower mortality rates from age sixty-five through one hundred.

Getting back to my Straight and Narrow participants, they may actually derive some health benefits from their sticking to a routine, although it's yet to be discovered whether their risk aversion creates other psychological problems. They may live longer, but will they feel more fulfilled? I'm reminded of researchers who study caloric restriction as a way to prolong life and who for years practice what they preach, only eventually to abandon their personal experiments when they find it's just not worth it to deny themselves life's simple pleasures. A longer life isn't all that desirable a goal if you spend that time feeling that you're trapped.

In fact, ample data from other researchers on work adjustment in the middle years of adulthood suggest that those who experience the greatest fulfillment in their careers are the ones who experiment with change and tinker in either a large or a small way to find the greatest congruence between themselves and their job conditions. Like my participants on the Authentic Road, who found a way to express their true selves in their work, those who are most successfully adjusted to their jobs in midlife have at least considered, if not acted upon, the desire to see what something else might feel like.

The topic of job change brings up a related issue pertaining to the central elements of vocational satisfaction. For many years, researchers in the area of work motivation believed in Frederick Herzberg's theory that the key to satisfaction lay in finding intrinsic motivation—the enjoyment of the work itself. Extrinsic motivation, the focus on salary and benefits, did not foster a deep ego involvement in one's occupation. This was a popular theory with bosses because it meant that they could pay people less, as long as they found a way to help them self-actualize. In my more cynical moments, I think that most educational and social service organizations are still based on this principle. However, the theory just didn't resonate with what the average person knows is true— that although money isn't the key to happiness, it helps in making life a lot more comfortable. So Herzberg's theory eventually faded in prominence.

Instead we now conceptualize work motivation in a more realistic way: Yes, jobs that are truly intrinsically rewarding engage our sense of identity and hence in the long run are more fulfilling than those we engage in only to earn a living. However, there are many shades between working for money and working for self-fulfillment. Edward Deci's self-determination theory, which asserts that our identities can get wrapped up in jobs even though those jobs have a strong extrinsic component, is now becoming increasingly used in the workplace. You can be a chef and really enjoy cooking and feel it expresses your true sense of self. But it's unlikely that you would keep this up forever if a paycheck never appeared.

Looking at the people in my sample, I agree that there was not a one-to-one correlation between pay and feelings of fulfillment. Think of Frank, the community development loan officer turned private financier. If anything, his high salary only made his situation seem more ironic and miserable to him. Conversely, Jerome gave up a comfortable and relatively prestigious position to fulfill his dream of becoming an archeologist. Although switching jobs isn't always the best way to achieve fulfillment, if it is done in a way that is deliberate, systematic, informed, and directed at satisfying your intrinsic needs, it can get you a long way toward that goal.

The final ingredient in the mix of midlife issues is relationships—not just romantic relationships but interconnections of all kinds. It's well-known in social psychology that having a strong social support network is one of the best buffers against negative emotional states such as depression and anxiety, particularly in later adulthood. But having people around and being involved with them are often two different things.

I'm thinking of how deeply embedded in their networks were Loretta and Arlene, two women on the Authentic Road. They seemed to draw strength from others. Relationships can also save us from spiraling downward, as was the case with Kathleen, whose adaptation was always tenuous at best but who seemed to have managed to stay afloat psychologically with the help of her older brother.

Relationships also include those we have with the younger generation. Clearly having your own kids provides you with the opportunity to make that direct connection. But being a parent is not a "gimme" to achieving fulfillment, particularly in the area of generativity. There were parents in my sample who did not have high levels of this quality, and childless participants who did. However, most of my participants actually were parents or stepparents. When everyone has the same quality, it's hard to examine its effects on participants. So in order to examine the role parenthood plays in fulfillment, I had to get a little creative and look at this variable not as a category (parent or nonparent) but in a different light.

After conducting a number of preliminary analyses, I arrived at a way of looking at the parenthood data in a manner that helped me identify a number of important patterns in people's lives. I noticed that some of the participants who showed the biggest jumps in generativity over the course of the study were those who became parents later in the game than was typical of this generation. This was another case where having longitudinal data really paid off; I knew what people were like before they were parents and I saw how they changed afterward.

A sophisticated statistical analysis, checked and rechecked with my University of Massachusetts colleague Aline Sayer, who is a national expert in the application of this tool, showed me that the people in my sample who became parents after their early thirties showed a continuous trajectory upward in their sense of generativity. I have referred to this in Chapter 2 as "catching up." It's not just that people higher in generativity were more likely to wait to have kids. Instead, my longitudinal data showed me that their generativity changed after they had their kids. Those who became parents in their twenties didn't show this same personality growth.

So I can't say that becoming a parent increases your sense of generativity, because almost everyone did become a parent. But I can say that if your kids come after you've consolidated some of your other life issues, you may very well find yourself more connected both to them and to their generation. These are the connections that keep you vital and engaged and will persist for decades to come.

What if you had your kids early? Are you fated to become disengaged from the young? Is it too late to change? I would say that the people who become parents in their twenties may find this kind of engagement more of a challenge, but I would also hope and believe that it's possible to feel connected. There are many ways to experience the fulfillment that comes with psychologically connecting to the young. It may seem trite to suggest this, but I truly believe that activities such as volunteering to teach, supporting a school extracurricular activity, and becoming a mentor are pretty good ways to fill the gaps in your sense of generativity.

Although many of the over-forty crowd may feel that the young are simply wastrels who do nothing but play video games, text message their friends, and drift around aimlessly, once you start to talk to these kids, you can find there's much more than meets the eye. I teach huge classes of first-year college students and I am always fascinated and often surprised to learn how mature their views on life can be even at their youthful ages, in their late teens. One kid in my class once remarked when describing an adverse situation in his personal life, "Well, it is what it is." I know that this has now become a somewhat clichéd remark, but after he told me about the situation he was referring to (his tough early years), I had to give him credit for having developed this existential philosophy from his real everyday experiences. In fact, a few days later I found myself uttering the phrase to myself when something wasn't going as I wished it would.

Children are not the key to fulfillment and on a day-to-day basis may make you feel that they are thwarting your developmental goals. (It's no fun to be told you're "embarrassing" or "annoying," after all.) But being willing to listen to them and engage with them psychologically can help form the foundation for your own continued growth.

What Is Midlife Growth?

I hope I've convinced you by now that our lives can't easily be segmented into chunks based on age, and that midlife in particular isn't marked by a shift in the tectonic plates that underlie the outward surface of our everyday comings and goings. Our lives are a mixture of growth and stability, the exact combination of which may occasionally be predictable but more often is not.

What do stand out, however, are our efforts to impose meaning on the seemingly chaotic events in our lives. We don't just walk blindly through the days and years that take us from youth to old age. We are constantly trying to make sense of what is happening to us even as our actions cause some of those things to happen. As I'll discuss in the next chapter, the order we try to impose is one that can allow us to look back at what we've done and allow us to prepare for what we will do in the future in order to maximize our impact on others. Our feelings of fulfillment will ultimately depend on whether we're able to put our lives into this healthy perspective.

CHAPTER 11

Legacy: The Key to Fulfillment

We spend much of our lives dealing with the day-to-day business of coping with everything from minor annoyances such as getting tied up in traffic to major stresses such as figuring out how to pay a child's college tuition or dealing with the illness of a relative or friend. Often we feel buffeted around by forces that seem at the moment to be completely out of our control. When in the course of our hectic lives do we have a chance to take stock and see whether what we're doing matters at all to anyone? Is it while waiting in line at the checkout counter at the grocery store or when we're trying to figure out where we left the car keys?

Although I spend a great deal of my own time involved in these mundane aspects of life (especially looking around for my car keys and other misplaced items), I suppose it's inevitable that I think about these larger issues pretty often, considering my particular profession and my particular research interests. I'm not exactly a philosopher, but I have pondered at length the factors that lead people in adulthood to feel that what they're doing is worth the effort. If nothing else, by studying the people in my sample, I've certainly been confronted with the question of what brings about happiness and fulfillment across the decades of adult life. Over the years, as I've observed the participants through the peaks and valleys of their personality development, I've come up with some thoughts about what ultimately leads all of us to feel fulfilled: It's coming to believe in the value of what we are doing with the time we have on this planet. The word that best captures this phenomenon is "legacy."

Where the Idea of Legacy Came From

When I began working on this book, I had just finished coediting with my colleague Sherry Willis an academic book on the baby boomers. We wrote the book with the intention of communicating to the world the latest scientific observations on this generation, as well as our own experiences. We thought that as boomers studying boomers we'd have fun working on the project and would be able to provide some useful insights as well. We were particularly interested in exploring the validity of some of the prevailing stereotypes about the current crop of mid-lifers and comparing the data with the myths.

It had always been my goal to portray the baby boomers the way that I have personally seen them. (I will use the third person from here on in, just for clarity, but by "them" I also mean "us.") And I have seen baby boomers in important ways in my own life, in the lives of my friends and colleagues, and by following the lives of my participants. I think that because I was close to the participants in age and had grown up close to their university, I felt as though I had a special kinship with them. When it came time to write the scientific articles based on my study, I always found it relatively easy to connect their personality changes both with the events in their lives and with the context in which their lives were playing out. I had a clear image in my mind of what many of them were like.

It was therefore with dismay that I witnessed the collapse of their scores on the ego integrity scale between their thirties and forties. In

Erikson's theory, ego integrity is supposed to become ascendant in later adulthood, and I had in fact already become convinced that this quality characterizes the majority of our years on this planet. We all need to believe that our lives have meaning, that we can accept our flaws, and that what we've done has made a difference to the lives of others. In later adulthood, our perspective is different from when we are younger, obviously, but these fundamental questions about our own existence concern us no matter our age. Since my sample's scores were headed downward, I feared there would not be good things in store for them over the next decade.

I wondered whether the lower ego integrity scores reflected the historical context rather than the collapse of my participants' inner psychological resources. After all, the younger generations I tracked also showed depressed scores on that scale. I had to assume that it was something in our society that was contributing to this pattern of scores.

Maybe there was hope for my generation after all. Maybe they weren't headed for existential deterioration. During the intervening decade between the third and fourth testings, various social changes took place, such as President Bill Clinton's call to volunteerism, that led me to think that my sample would perhaps show a spike in their scores at the next testing. I was optimistic that a wave of selflessness could replace the widespread selfishness of the 1980s. If this could trickle down the way that trickle-down economics never did, maybe my participants (and my generation) would be rescued from a bitter and isolated old age.

I had many reasons for optimism, besides reading the winds of social change. After all, the baby boomers were at the forefront of the activism of the 1960s, challenging racism and sexism. (A third "ism," ageism, is one they are challenging now.) And for many in this generation, the spirit of volunteerism was awakened in the 1960s by the words and acts of President John F. Kennedy and the members of his administration who established community service organizations that are still going strong.

Again, we have to be careful not to lump everyone into the same category, but I think it's safe to say that the baby boomers did make the world a better place. Just think about the first Earth Day, on April 22, 1970, which paved the way for what would become a globalized effort to work toward ensuring the future of our planet. The ecology movement was spearheaded by the many college students who worked to bring that effort to fruition.

Thus, early on in the process of analyzing the data I collected when my sample was in their midfifties, I realized that it would be important to look for variations from person to person in patterns of change, and not just generation-level trends. Ego integrity was the personality dimension that interested me the most, precisely because of its role as an indicator of mental health. Eventually, along with overall life satisfaction, it became my prime focus as I identified the pathways. I first classified people according to a combination of these two scores, as an index of self-fulfillment, and then I went on to try to understand why the individuals had received the scores they did.

As I tried to make sense of the varying patterns of scores in the thirty-four years of the study, I suddenly found myself thinking about the concept of legacy. I suppose I had been reading the stories in the media on legacy in its economic sense. Plenty of news broadcasts run features about how the millions of retiring baby boomers are hoping to ensure that their children and grandchildren will gain an inheritance. But it would turn out to be a different kind of legacy that would determine fulfillment and happiness for the men and women in my study.

What I noticed about my participants with high self-fulfillment scores was not that they had necessarily left behind economic security, although some of them surely had. What was more important was that they were involved in endeavors that took them outside of their own, more narrowly defined concerns of personal comfort. To me, this was the hallmark of a psychological legacy. There was ample evidence that these people were volunteering their time (not just donating cash) for local charities, engaging in educational projects, and getting involved in other causes spanning a wide range of public interest concerns. Some of the participants had even corresponded with me during the follow-up from 2000 to 2002, to share with me how important it was to them to be able to contribute to this study.

The most psychologically healthy among them were shown in their other test scores to be nondefensive, interested in the welfare of others, able to establish emotional commitments, willing to work hard, and confident in their own identities. In other words, they had reached a healthy maturity characterized by self-acceptance and a social interest that extended beyond their own personal concerns. These were the real "legacy builders."

I've come to understand legacy in this psychological sense as the feeling that what you are doing in life is making a difference for others, particularly for those of the generations that will come after you. In and of itself, the term "legacy" is value-neutral. Although for the most part we tend to think of legacy as a good thing, to be technical about it, people can have all kinds of legacies. A dictator like Hitler or Stalin leaves a legacy of devastation and murder throughout the country he terrorizes. A U.S. president whose effect on the world is not quite as outright horrific can still have a legacy whose value is debatable. Think of a Herbert Hoover, or even Richard Nixon.

I would argue, though, that it's the positive type of legacy tied in with normal and healthy personality functioning that is the key, ultimately, to achieving self-fulfillment. I suppose this implies a sort of moral judgment, because to say that a legacy is "positive" means that it has contributed something of worth or goodness. Who's to decide what's worthwhile and good? To get to this side of the argument, I have to dip into several relevant theories of personality and development.

One such theory is based on the very useful but not widely publicized work of the Washington University psychologist Jane Loevinger, who for over thirty years wrote extensively about the development of personality as growth of character. To understand how our sense of self (the ego) develops, the theory goes, we also have to understand the development of our thought processes. She proposed that we all go through a series of increasingly mature stages that begin with the notion of right and wrong as an all-or-none, black-and-white set of distinctions. As we gain in maturity, we become better able to see reality as complex and multidimensional. If we reach the highest stage, which unfortunately few people do, we achieve true realization of our "inner self."

Loevinger's ideas are reminiscent of the ideas of late Harvard psychologist Lawrence Kohlberg, known for his theory that we go through a set of stages in moral development that allow us to move increasingly away from a "law and order" orientation to a more complex sense of right and wrong. Kohlberg proposed that at the highest stage of morality, we appreciate the value of human life above all else.

Humanistic psychology, which I mentioned before in my discussion of Maslow and Rogers, also emphasizes the positive nature of what we can contribute to the lives of others through our own actions. For many years, this branch of psychology referred to itself as the "third force" in psychology, emphasizing free will and countering the deterministic theories of behaviorism and psychoanalysis. I suppose it's fair to say that humanistic psychology provided the intellectual roots of the current positive psychology movement.

For its part, Freud's psychodynamic theory didn't completely ignore the human need to make positive contributions to society and the world. Alfred Adler, a disciple of Freud's until their theories no longer fit comfortably in with each other, proposed that humans have a fundamental need to contribute to the good of society. Adlerians today still teach the importance of social values, caring for children, and getting along with the community as a whole. Having these social values promoting that we work alongside others in a cooperative way rather than, in his words, "striving for superiority" over others, provides an important component of the healthy personality.

Even if we feel uncomfortable deciding on an objective basis whether someone has contributed in a "positive" manner to society, we can in any case agree that when we evaluate the meaning of our life's work, we do so on the basis of the social values we have incorporated into our sense of ethics as we've grown up.

In the interview study on midlife I completed with Dannefer

(mentioned in Chapter 10), I asked participants a set of questions dealing with their personal values. I don't think there was a single individual who claimed to take pride in being dishonest or unethical. It was quite the contrary. Most people try to see themselves as honest and good, and will go through a large variety of mental twists and turns to ensure that they can preserve this favorable self-view. From a pragmatic standpoint, then, we can conclude that if we are making contributions that our society values, we will be more likely to view our legacies in a positive manner. It is on that basis, if not on a philosophical basis, that I consider the kind of legacy that matters to be one that is oriented toward favorable social goals.

All of these positions informed my underlying assumption when examining the lives of the people in my sample. I concluded that the desire to leave a positive legacy is a fundamental motivation that in turn serves as the ultimate basis for self-fulfillment. I then tried to understand the very important question as to why some people were able to reach the goal of establishing a legacy and achieving fulfillment and others were not.

With this framework in mind, I began to try to identify the factors that led people to be able or unable to leave a legacy. I first looked at people who clearly felt that their search for legacy had failed. I suppose it was the clinical psychologist in me trying to learn from what goes wrong in order to find out what can go right. By gaining a perspective on what didn't work out well for these participants, I could later understand how and why others succeeded. The most striking cases of these unfulfilled legacy seekers were people who, by all objective accounts, "should" have felt fulfilled. They had families, successful jobs, and were well-respected in respectable communities. However, as I dug more deeply into their psychological profiles, I gained insight into why they looked back on their accomplishments with such despair.

I think that of all the participants, it was Frank, the mortgage-loan executive, who most typified this pattern and thus engaged my attention. His life had deviated from his youthful goal of developing public housing and retail properties in underprivileged communities. In late midlife, he could not look back on what he'd done with pride. Instead he felt that he had abandoned his earlier visions of contributing to the public good, in favor of actions that would benefit him financially and professionally.

I learned from Frank that in order to leave a legacy, you need to know what your internal value system is and you need to be able to orient yourself so that this system is expressed through your life's accomplishments.

Fulfilling what you regard as your central mission in life can also serve to inspire others. You become a role model, and then some. By showing that it's possible to overcome adversity, for example, as was true for those on the Triumphant Trail, we can help lift other people's spirits when they feel weighted down by the burdens of their own tribulations. A legacy in such a case can take the form of knowing that we've helped others, even at the cost of our own suffering. When we are victims of extremely stressful life events, we can derive some comfort, after the events have passed, in knowing that we've provided a model of adaptation.

For instance, a news program staple is the filming of the parents of deceased children talking about the focus their lives have taken, as they fight against whatever condition caused their children's death, be it cancer, crime, or reckless driving. These people certainly didn't choose this path to creating a legacy, but once life dealt them this particular blow, they turned their anguish into socially productive contributions that could quite literally serve to prevent the same misfortune from happening to others.

Reacting to adversity is one thing, but creating your own adversity is quite another. Here I'm referring to the people on the Downward Slope. I'd like to return to the case of Barbara, whose story you read about in the opening pages of the book. You heard about the main features of her life—her successful career as an engineer, her failed (in her opinion) career as a wife. I was truly puzzled and frustrated by Barbara's life story. Objectively speaking, her legacy in the world has been clearly established. She has served as a model for other female engineers and scientists, made important discoveries, and helped solve big problems. These solutions not only benefit the scientific enterprise but also have practical value. We might even wonder how we could fairly put her in the Downward Slope category.

The reason is that, as successful as she was, her inner torment and failure to achieve fulfillment dominated her inner existence. Barbara's case shows us the extreme disconnect that can occur when a person who very literally is leaving behind a positive legacy fails to believe that she is doing so. To explain this disconnect, I have to hypothesize that she at some level blames herself for not being a success all around but "only" a success in her work.

I also have reason to believe that adding to this sense of failure as a married woman might be resentment of her situation as a female scientist. It's a good bet that she has encountered a significant degree of sexism, perhaps in the form of receiving a lower salary than her male colleagues (the terror of the "gender gap") or being offered fewer opportunities for promotion. There is considerable prejudice within the scientific establishment against women, and there certainly was even more of it when Barbara began her career.

Recently one of my undergrad students told me a chilling tale of her first day attending an advanced math class at the university. Her professor made it clear that she and the other three women in the class (out of a class of thirty) would undoubtedly do poorly in the course, and throughout the semester he did everything he could to ensure that this outcome would come to pass. Luckily, the student not only succeeded in the class but went on to a prestigious graduate program with full funding, probably much to his annoyance. If nothing else, being treated as a second-class citizen can, over time, erode your self-confidence, no matter how many objective indicators of your success there are for you to see. It takes an unusual person to avoid being dragged down by such negative treatment.

The one positive sign in Barbara's case, which may in fact allow her to embrace her legacy eventually, is that despite it all she has managed to show a great deal of positive growth over the decades. On everything but ego integrity, she's a lot better off than she was in her twenties. If she can overcome the regret she feels about her past mistakes and focus on how much she has objectively accomplished, there is hope for her to reach fulfillment.

Up to this point, I have treated legacy in a sort of "writ large" manner, looking at the big picture of a person's overall contributions and the feelings of inner satisfaction that those contributions can bring. But I think it's important to avoid falling into the trap of seeing legacy only as a function of achieving some sort of fame or making a notable addition to the world. We can't all be da Vinci, Einstein, or Lincoln. We can't even all get our fifteen minutes of fame. So what about the average person whose realm of influence is relatively narrow? Is there any hope of legacy for him or her?

The answer is that legacies come in all shapes and sizes. For example, we like to think that even if we don't accomplish everything we want to in our own lives, we will produce children who will themselves achieve some form of greatness. But here again, it's not necessary for our children to become Nobel scientists, great world leaders, or Olympic athletes in order for us to feel that we have fulfilled our roles of raising them successfully. Living our own lives well can lead us to produce children who are compassionate and well-adjusted. And then, of course, there are grandchildren, a truly visible sign of our legacy lasting far beyond our own lives or even those of our kids. Here again, though, is only one form of legacy. It isn't necessary to have descendents in order to have a lineage.

There are a variety of mini-routes to legacy that individually may not seem like much but that taken together allow you to feel that your life is adding up to something worthwhile. For example, maybe you bake an outstanding apple pie, one that is so remarkable that friends and family beg you to share the recipe with them. You can take satisfaction in the fact that whenever someone bakes that pie in the future, you will be remembered as its creator. As a matter of fact, I have a few recipes like that in my very tattered recipe box, some going back to my early twenties. Every time I make the chili recipe given to me by one of my fellow students, I think about her—not only what a great cook she was but how much fun we had together swapping stories about the agonies of grad school. Now my younger daughter has learned that recipe, and so the legacy of Laurie's great chili has been clearly established.

A mini-route to legacy may occur quite serendipitously. Think about the effect that other people have had on you during situations when you least expected it. For instance, have you ever had an encounter with a stranger who said something that touched a deep nerve within you? Some of us have had our most in-depth (if also annoying) conversations sharing a claustrophobic ride on an airplane with a person we are confident we will never see again. We tend to exchange highly personal information, with the assumption that we're safe because the person doesn't even know our name, or certainly not our last name. The chances are good that the person is someone entirely out of our social network. So in addition to having a chance to get your problems off your chest, for the moment, you may have gotten a totally new view on one of your life's chronic problems.

As you go through life, there are countless other even smaller ways in which your actions also "stick" in the minds of others. Perhaps you've had the wonderful experience of someone telling you what an impact you had on their life, an impact that may have been completely unintended. Perhaps an acquaintance was struggling with a family problem such as an irresponsible teenager and you mentioned that you knew someone who might be able to hook that kid up with an after-school volunteer program. Now instead of hanging with his friends and getting up to no good, this kid is using his energy to help others, thanks to your passing comment.

Your legacy can also include the part of yourself that continues on in the minds of others. Perhaps it's a story with an object lesson that you've been told by a grandparent that you pass along to your own children, which they in turn will carry forward into the future generations. Your grandmother's story was incorporated into your own worldview, establishing that piece of her legacy within you. Now, as you pass the tale down to those who are younger, you are sharing your storehouse of knowledge, which then becomes part of your legacy to them.

The psychologist Paul Baltes defined "wisdom" with the somewhat dense phrase "knowledge in the pragmatics of everyday life." This means that people who are wise have acquired a perspective that allows them to help others figure out how to tackle some of life's most difficult challenges. For example, perhaps your grandmother struggled and overcame the challenges of supporting and raising her children while living with an alcoholic husband. Not only can you learn from the example she set, but you can also learn from her valuable insights into how to develop your own inner resolve during the hard times in your life. Her legacy of wisdom becomes incorporated into the way you make decisions and ultimately becomes incorporated into what you pass on to others.

In your work, your legacy can take many forms. You do not have to be in what we normally think of as a "helping" profession to leave a legacy. You can be a construction worker, a dental hygienist, an accountant, a lawyer, or a bank manager. There are practical and lasting products you can leave behind no matter what your field of endeavor. And even more important is the feeling that you've done something useful with whatever skills and abilities you possess.

By the same token, being in a mentoring or helping occupation doesn't provide a sure ticket to your legacy. I know plenty of people, unfortunately, who serve in an instructional capacity such as teaching or advising students who are burned out and uninvolved in the lives of those they are supposed to be helping. Perhaps as an ironic tribute to the prominence of burnout in academia, an administrator on my campus (who himself sadly became a victim of burnout) insisted on placing signs around the dorms proclaiming "Students First!" I found it hard to fathom the meaning of these signs, but I suppose it testified to the fact that even those whose primary job is to educate the young may need to be reminded of their mission.

Evaluating Your Legacy

Project into the future fifty or one hundred years from now, and imagine that someone comes across your name in a family record book, a history of your corporation, or, if they can still access the media, a digital image of you. Or perhaps someone is listening to a piece of music you composed, reading a poem you wrote, or staring at a piece of art you painted. Maybe it's that chili recipe that they find stuck in the back of a passed-down family cookbook. Where would you most want and hope your name to be found?

Next, evaluate how far along you have come toward accomplishing that for which you would like to be remembered. Given that we can't necessarily predict how our accomplishments will be regarded in the future, we can at least take our cues from the impact we are having on others now. If you want to be remembered as someone who gave wise advice to others, think about the number of times people have thanked you for helping them through a crisis. If you are hoping to be seen as the next Emily Dickinson, your validation may be a little harder to achieve or take some decades or more. In the meantime, there are many ways that you can experience the pleasure of feeling you've done something worthwhile.

During this process it's advisable to be realistic overall, but there are times when it helps to focus on the positive. Just think of Barbara, who emphasized the failures in her relationships rather than the successes in her profession. You could unnecessarily be torturing yourself for not having accomplished something relating to your weaker qualities, instead of choosing to focus on a legacy that plays to your strengths.

Still, it's important to realize that our legacy isn't something we often consciously contemplate. People who are still in their early adult or even midlife years rarely stop everything they're doing to ask these questions outright. Even people later along in life may not spend much time consciously thinking about their overall purpose and whether or not they've met it. At some level, it might not even be all that healthy to sit around and think about whether you're self-fulfilled.

There is a concept called "flow" that refers to being able to perform effortlessly at your peak. Sports psychologists warn their clients about how easy it is for flow to be interrupted, causing calamitous consequences. Once you start to break down what you're doing and think about it, you miss the shot, drop the ball, or trip over your feet. The same might hold true with legacy, at least to an extent.

On that point, I'm reminded of one of the very earliest research projects I completed on the topic of ego integrity. My doctoral student at the time, Maxine Walaskay, was also a pastoral counselor at the university. She and I developed a project for her dissertation in which she interviewed about forty older adults to evaluate their personality development. She used a test we developed to examine the relationship of ego integrity to other qualities related to end-of-life issues such as fear of death. For example, the questionnaire included items asking participants if they had made plans for their funerals.

To our surprise, some of the most successfully adapted people in the study had not gone through a "crisis" of evaluating their life's meaning or contributions (part of ego integrity) at all. Nevertheless, they had remarkably high scores in feelings of satisfaction with their life accomplishments. In terms of their mortality, contrary to our expectations, they gave the existential issues regarding their death very little thought. However, they had figured out who would be invited to their funerals and even what they wanted to be dressed in as they lay in the coffin. Death to them was less a question of coming to grips with mortality than deciding on whether they should be clad in their finest blue silk suit or their most stylish plaid.

These individuals had achieved ego integrity, were low in fear of death, and high on the scale measuring their acceptance of life. What about our theory that in order to achieve ego integrity one must have gone through an existential crisis? We could only propose that for some people, feeling fulfilled does not require that they scrutinize closely the very depth of life's meaning.

Similarly, I doubt if everyone in my sample who felt they'd left something of importance for future generations would regard this as a major aspect of their psychological life. In other words, they may not have labeled themselves as "legacy builders."

So if things are going well, you don't necessarily have to set aside "legacy time" each day, or even each week, or even each year. If you are feeling fulfilled with what you're doing, and you happen to notice that people react to you in ways that suggest you are making a difference in their lives, then don't interrupt the flow. Instead, question the status quo once in a while, perhaps, especially when you feel that you're getting stuck in meaningless pursuits.

And if you truly wonder whether you've done anything with your life other than leave a huge carbon footprint, if you notice that people are treating you as irrelevant (and you feel irrelevant), or if you keep making decisions that cause you more pain than pleasure, why not take stock? You might be afraid to learn what the outcome is because the inertia of your situation is keeping you comfortably hewn in. But the alternative is far worse: If you don't address these questions now, you may never have the courage to ask them again, or you may not see a way out of your circumstances later on. Without being too impulsive, you'll want to give yourself that chance to make the adjustments now, so that you can start building a legacy you'll be proud of.

CHAPTER 12

The Pathway Ahead

The pathway your life follows can lead you toward or away from fulfillment. Ideally, your pathway will carry you through to those feelings of inner fulfillment. The key is figuring out how you got onto your pathway. And then, if you're not moving in the right direction, figure out how to redirect yourself so that you can become fulfilled. If your pathway is going where you want it to, you've seen by now that it still takes effort to keep things moving in a positive direction. So, if you'd like to stay on your pathway, I'll help you do that. And if not, I'll help you navigate a shift to a more fulfilling pathway.

Throughout the book, you've seen examples of people who have made changes in their life paths. We're led to believe that as we get older, we become more set in our ways. However, people can and do make significant changes in midlife and beyond. Stories abound in the media of elderly people who go back to school. Actually, in 2007 the oldest recipient of a college degree was Nola Ochs, who graduated from Fort Hays State University in Kansas at the age of ninety-five. Hers is an extreme case, but she shows us that it's not impossible to turn your life around if you're dissatisfied with it, regardless of your age.

It is true that some of us carry out the patterns of our early years for decades, but still many others are able to shuck off their past and start fresh. By looking at the life pathways of people who extricate themselves from unhappy circumstances, you can get ideas about how to change your life pathways to maximize your fulfillment now. You'll find that you don't have to be stuck with an unhappy job, family situation, or even personality.

Conduct a Life Review

Earlier in the book, I mentioned the life review, a concept invented by psychiatrist Robert Butler (the inventor of the term "ageism"). The life review involves the very simple, or one might say "deceptively simple," task of comparing what you've done in your life with what you hoped you would do. The next step is reconciling those differences and allowing yourself to accept the life you have lived.

This exercise might sound like one for your deathbed. That is actually close to what Butler intended. He based the idea on Erikson's concept of ego integrity, which he associated with the advanced later years of life. Older adults in a state of despair, according to Butler, needed a way to work through the pain of their failures and come to accept and integrate all parts of themselves and their lives into a unified whole, by way of reminiscence.

For many years, gerontologists had asserted that it was unhealthy for older adults to dwell on the past. "Reality orientation" was the buzz word for geriatric treatment in the late 1970s. Keep older people focused on the present or they will drift off into a haze of confusion, was the mantra uttered by workers in the field. It was Butler who first pointed out that older adults in particular have to be given a chance to reconcile their past mistakes and failings in order to make peace with their mortality.

I thought the idea of the life review made a great deal of sense, and I particularly agreed with Butler's proposal that reminiscence can serve an adaptive function as we get older. But I also wondered why it couldn't be used earlier in life. Couldn't everyone benefit from a little bit of "pre" reminiscing? In other words, as young adults we can imagine how as older adults we will look back on the current times. Or what about the times we've done something that's resulted in someone else being hurt or angry? Why should we wait until we're older to come to grips with our past mistakes? Why not try to fix them now? Or even better, avoid making them in the first place by thinking ahead?

Sometimes it's a matter of listening to your gut feeling that tells you that you might be in danger if you take certain actions. The Swiss psychiatrist Carl Jung, whom I discussed in the context of Loretta's story in Chapter 9, pointed out that we need a balance in our lives between the opposing factors in our personalities, a process he called "individuation." He also had another idea that hardheaded empiricists regard as a bit off the wall—that our unconscious can sometimes tell when our lives have gotten out of balance, a phenomenon that he referred to as "synchronicity" or a "meaningful association" between seemingly unrelated events.

Perhaps in your waking life you are overly stressed, for example—as many of us are—so stressed that you take to doing something you know you shouldn't, namely, reading your email on your cellphone while you're driving or, worse, responding to an email while you're driving. Let's say you have a dream that you've been in a terrible car accident. Jung would say that your unconscious "knew" that you were putting yourself at risk and is telling you to stop. In his book *Man and His Symbols*, Jung cited several cases of clients' dreams that presaged calamitous outcomes.

So, according to Jung, our unconscious may know that trouble is brewing. Even if you don't believe that your unconscious can predict events, though, everyone can cite an instance when a little warning bell went off in their head before they made a terrible decision. It could be anything from a bad investment to the decision not to break up with a romantic partner who was clearly exploiting or manipulating you. You ignored the intuition and lived to regret it.

If you had engaged in "pre" reminiscing, you would have taken that warning and explored it before acting. You would have projected ahead into the future and imagined how that decision would have played out. If your crystal ball had showcased serious problems, then you would have taken a step back.

I'm also talking about impulse control here, the ability to stop before making a hasty decision. There's good evidence that people who age successfully are the ones who manage to avoid a lot of impulsive decisions, which is partly why they are still healthy and alive long enough to make it to their sixties, seventies, and beyond.

Of course, it's not always possible to avoid poor life decisions or negative life events, no matter how cautiously you plan or how wisely you project into the future. When that happens, it's natural to wish that you could relive the moment when everything started to fall apart and alter it to make everything come out all right.

In Chapter 4, I talked about the movie *Groundhog Day,* in which the main character relives a particular day in his life over and over again until he is finally able to avoid making the mistakes that would set his life off course. Real life doesn't give us true opportunities to engage in this type of reparative work. However, when we see that a situation is spinning out of control, we can intervene before the results become truly disastrous. Using the life review proactively is one way to accomplish that goal.

Cut Your Losses and Move On

Recall my participant whose website bore this sage advice about recouping from a bad decision. You can also use the life review even while the events in your life are occurring. Rather than wait, then you'll be able to move on without allowing a particularly negative experience to haunt you for years, if not decades.

I'm reminded of the story of one of my participants whose life started to unravel after one particularly unfortunate incident, one that

I'm sure he wishes he could relive and change. On the basis of his outstanding pitching performance with his college baseball team, Jack was given a chance to play for the pros when he graduated from the university. Here was the opportunity he must have dreamed of all his life. Sure enough, after two seasons in which he progressed from a minor league farm team to the majors, Jack seemed destined for a solid position in the pitching rotation of an expansion team for at least the next three or four years.

Miraculously, the team had accumulated a winning record that had put them only one game away from the play-offs. It was Jack's big night to make it happen. However, fate wasn't kind, and under the intense pressure, his pitching imploded. The events of that night, though thirty years ago, are still documented by grumbling fans writing on the Internet, just as Red Sox fans still bemoan the infamous Mike Torrez–Bucky Dent incident that cost them the chance to play in the World Series in 1978. Batter Dent, playing for the Yankees, homered against Torrez in the fateful game, extending the Red Sox curse.

His own gruesome night was the kiss of death for Jack, not only in the major (and minor) league from then on but for the remainder of his work career. As I traced through his string of failures in the business world, where he seemed to have been fired from a series of positions in insurance sales, I sadly detected the pattern of the Downward Slope. What struck me about Jack's case was the suddenness with which everything fell apart, all of which I traced to that one game.

If you are sympathizing with Jack—and who wouldn't be—you probably have that same wish in the back of your mind, that he could relive that night and make it all turn out perfectly. Perhaps you've had an event like this occur to you, where something you did or said instantly changed your fate. Rationally, we know that we can't change history, but we all like to play around with the idea from time to time, especially when a key misstep sent us in a bad direction.

Here again the life review can come in handy. You can't change the past, so what about learning a new way to think about the event? If you recast it in a way that allows you to see how it contributed to your growth as a person, or if you can find a silver lining in there somewhere, you don't have to spend the rest of your life filled with bitterness and regret.

I'm not sure what it would take for Jack to feel better about his botched performance that night. He was probably told all the usual palliative things by his friends and family, if not by his coach or manager, although my guess is that he was fired soon after. I'm sure at some level he knew he was going to have to shake it off to move on with his life.

Had he engaged in a proactive life review, though, Jack could have seen his situation from a broader perspective. He could have re-examined his goals for the future and thought about what he wanted to accomplish in the coming decades. And at the same time, he could have planned on new ways to express his identity, ones that would allow him ultimately to look back on his life with feelings of fulfillment.

Compose Your Own Life Story

Butler's work on the life review stimulated me to begin a research program on reminiscence, where my colleagues and I looked at the ways in which thinking back on the past, its positive *and* negative aspects, could enhance ego integrity in older adults. In the process, I began to think about the types of narratives that people form about their lives, what I ended up calling the "life story," based on an influential piece of writing by a psychoanalytic life span colleague named Bertram Cohler. It seemed to me that the adults who'd aged the most successfully had managed to compose an autobiography that had worked through the negative events in their lives in such a way that the events were no longer viewed as entirely detrimental. Their "life stories" tended to portray the subjects as having successfully conquered their challenges.

The counterpart to the life story is what I call the "life scenario," which is the script that young people build of how they see their futures unfolding. Our visions of the future when we are young are an extension of our sense of self. As we develop our identities, we begin to spin out future scenarios for ourselves.

What was your scenario? Perhaps you saw yourself as heading toward success in business and planned to have achieved a position of prominence as a top Fortune 500 executive. Maybe your goals were in the area of public service and you dreamed of yourself as a politician or government official who would be able to make a difference in the world. Perhaps you wanted to become a musician, entertainer, or artist whose work would lead to widespread renown. Instead, though, you are leading an average life, important perhaps within your own social networks but not far beyond the realm of those who have known you for years. Or perhaps you are frustrated because you haven't been able to make an impact in areas that you think would benefit from your particular talents.

Clearly Jack's life scenario was that he would be a star athlete. When things didn't work out that way for him, he might have changed the scenario to project himself into the future not as the next Cy Young but as a star insurance salesperson. My sense is that his heart (and identity) was not in it. Had he been able to project a future in which he was a success in business, I think he would have been okay.

Then, working backward later in life as he wrote his life story, Jack might have seen his two years as a pro athlete as an exciting time that he truly enjoyed but that unfortunately ended in one bad night. Over time, he might even have engaged in a little harmless self-deception and started to alter his memory of his last game so that the focus shifted to factors not entirely within his control (bad weather, a poorly fitting glove, an unusually talented bunch of opposing batters). Interestingly, Red Sox pitcher Torrez seemed to have been able to overcome his own brush with destiny; he's quoted as saying, "Don't blame me. I did my job. . . . It never changed my life."

As it was, though, my participant Jack couldn't find it within himself to make those rewrites. I would guess that at his core he started to form an identity as a "loser," a self-image made even more poignant when he contrasted his rising star in college with the precipitous drop that he took only a couple of years later. Once his "loser" identity was fully formed, he found getting his life back on track to become an almost insurmountable challenge.

Rewriting a chapter in your own life story isn't a process that is quickly accomplished. And it's not necessarily a great idea simply to gloss it over, even though to do so might cause the pain to go away more quickly. Instead you need to look at the experience from all angles, particularly while it is still fresh in your mind, before poor memory has had a chance to obstruct your ability to view it clearly. What was your role in contributing to the negative outcome? Was it an argument where hurtful words were exchanged? Was it an accident or other misfortune that you caused in which someone was injured? Or did you fail to take advantage of an opportunity or in some other way limit your ability to succeed by making a stupid decision?

As you ask yourself these questions, it might be painful to produce honest answers, but that self-scrutiny is step one in revising the event in your mental diary. At some point after that, you have to move on to step two, in which you try to derive positive meaning from the event, make amends to whomever you hurt, or simply soften the hard edges around the images still pervading your consciousness. If appropriate, a little humor can't hurt either. If you can poke fun at yourself or at least start to see the ridiculousness of a ridiculous situation, it can go a long way toward moving the healing process along.

Finally, you're ready to start the revision process. You can't wipe the event out of your mind, but you can begin to frame it as having become a part of who you are now—flawed but still "you." If possible, and if life and death consequences were not involved (which clearly make the process more complicated), you can actively try to do what many psychologically healthy individuals seem to do quite naturally: minimize their role in failure and instead start to shift some of the culpability onto the other people involved in the situation.

If it was an argument that resulted in the end of a relationship, you can begin to allow the memories to fade of the damaging things you said and instead let the other person's words come into sharper relief so you can put yours into context. Eventually, having gotten what you can out of the process in terms of your own personal growth (such as promising that you will be more patient or more humble), you can move on and recategorize the experience as one where there was a 50-50 sharing of blame.

Jack's ability to leave a positive legacy behind is yet to be determined. I hope that he will eventually integrate the past difficulties he has faced and through the process arrive at an outlook that substitutes his feelings of discouragement and failure with acceptance. Donning my clinical hat for a moment, I think undergoing psychotherapy would be the best way for him to start to turn things around, because by now the loser identity is so entrenched. Then I would strongly urge him to find a way to use the life experiences he's had as a basis for helping others. Why not coach a Little League or softball team? How about taking what he's learned from the business world and teach part-time in a community college or adult education program? My study showed that it's not enough to just elevate your feelings of happiness in order to achieve a legacy—you also have to do something to pass along to others your skills, experience, care, and concern.

Find Your Legacy

As I pointed out in the previous chapter, there are many routes to legacy, and not all of them involve making contributions recognized on a worldwide scale. Your life story doesn't have to be an epic novel. It can be a short story, or even a series of short stories—small accomplishments that add up to a life that you, and others, consider to have been well-lived.

Consider the life story of Jean, my top scorer on the ego integrity scale. When I looked at her accomplishments, I wasn't exactly blown away by her résumé. In fact, it all seemed fairly ordinary. But for some reason, her ego integrity score had nearly maxed out at the uppermost value, and her other personality scales were also very strong. Somehow she'd found a formula for personal gratification. What could I learn from her?

I'm pretty certain Jean wasn't trying to make herself look good just for the sake of looking good. That's always a question in my mind when I see someone with such a favorable profile. The reason is that she actually admitted that, overall, she was "satisfied" with her life, not "very satisfied," which was the highest score possible. She evidently still had some goals she was hoping to meet, or maybe she was working through some other issues.

Like many of the women of her generation, Jean chose a career in the traditionally female profession of nursing. A few years after beginning her job, she went back to school for a master's degree, which she completed part-time. Again, a fairly typical route for someone of her gender and time. She married a hospital personnel administrator in her midtwenties and started her family a few years after that. Jean's life was, again, so far rather unremarkable. In college, her personality scores were solid, but like many of her peers, she wasn't over-the-top industrious.

Over the course of her thirties and forties, Jean continued to show favorable personality growth, with gains in every area, though not to equal degrees and not to the max on any one scale. It was in the area of ego integrity, however, that she would eventually shine, earning the top spot in the sample.

How did she develop such a favorable assessment of her life? What role did legacy play in that process? Nursing might seem to be one of those natural legacy-building professions, but as I've pointed out, it's not occupation alone that qualifies someone as establishing a positive legacy. In fact, one of the unhappiest women in the sample, with one of the lowest ego integrity scores possible, was a nurse. There were also plenty of people in full-time teaching roles (another legacy-friendly occupation, one would think) whose ego integrity scores were on the negative side.

I had to conclude that Jean hadn't built a legacy exclusively through her job. I could even argue that jobs such as nursing and teaching can have a counter-effect toward legacy building, given their attendant risks of stress and burnout. Add in the low pay given to people in these crucially important professions, and you've got a formula for bitterness and cynicism rather than self-actualization. Fortunately, I think most of the people who gravitate toward those jobs actually find ways to avoid the burnout, or at least that was the case with those in my sample.

Jean's secret seems to lie in what she did with her time when she was not at work. After seeing the tough conditions under which many of her fellow workers performed their duties, Jean had become active in the local health care workers union. Eventually her efforts paid off—she was elected president. Now in addition to her already demanding job, Jean commits considerable extra time to this volunteer post. I imagine she has spent many long days and late nights away from her family.

Jean didn't stop there. She also volunteered at one of the local high schools. It just so happened that the school had a very successful glee club that needed help with various administrative duties associated with their travels. Proving the motto "If you want something done, ask a busy person," Jean also served effectively in this role. Having been involved in the extracurricular scene when my own kids were in school, I know how these things happen. It starts out with an innocent enough offer to help out with one event, but it eventually turns into something you find so rewarding that you're doing far more than you'd expected. Jean continued her work even after her own children were no longer directly involved with the program. She had found it intrinsically motivating to spend time with young people even if it was not going to directly benefit her own family.

There are many possible reasons why Jean feels so elated about her life, in contrast to Jack, who feels so bitter and resentful. I wouldn't necessarily claim cause and effect—that good works lead to feelings of self-fulfillment—but Jean is active in ways that are germane to the notion of legacy. Helping others in her work and helping others in her spare time seems to me like a pretty good formula for fulfillment.

If we look back on the lives of some of the people in my sample who achieved self-fulfillment even though they suffered from misfortune, a mistake, or a set of rough life conditions, we can point to legacy as the key. In contrast to those on the Downward Slope, these were the people who moved increasingly upward with each passing year. And as that happened, their inner strength continued to bulk up to prepare them for whatever might lie ahead.

If, like Jack, you have not done so well, then your chances of successfully adapting to later adulthood will be severely hampered. How can you shed the past and move more favorably into your later years? One way to approach this time period with a positive attitude is to, like Jean, make worthwhile contributions to society through your work. People like Jean who feel good about themselves and their lives also tend to accept the mistakes they make without dwelling on them.

And rather than being preoccupied with their own personal needs, a number of people in my study moved toward ego integrity by helping others—giving them guidance, support, or opportunities to improve themselves.

As I noted already, it's all too easy to get drawn into the "generation gap" mentality and complain that the young aren't worth your time. But keep in mind that, as we saw with Julia, the mentoring you provide to the young performs a vitally important service. The benefit to you is that your care and attention to younger family members or colleagues helps your own personality growth as well. Think about who in your life did (or did not) help you, and that should motivate you even further.

Unfortunately, many middle-aged people feel threatened that they will be supplanted by the young. Instead of welcoming new people into their organizations or professions, these insecure midlife adults become defensive of their positions and try to resist what they see as encroachment. They try to protect their prestige by throwing more obstacles in front of young people trying to get ahead, or, just as bad, they ignore them.

For their part, the young are easily intimidated by older and more accomplished people. Remember the way you felt when you were new to your job and you were at meetings with senior staff or supervisors. Only the most courageous young person will seek ways to be heard if the elders don't give that person permission to speak. Break this pattern by giving young people leadership positions and then mentoring them so that they can be successful in carrying out their assignments.

Avoid the Anti-Aging Trap

Another way to enhance your sense of fulfillment is to look at the way you spend both your money and energy. Baby boomer women (and men, to a lesser extent) are now the target of an entire anti-aging industry trying to peddle everything from plastic surgery in a bottle to "beautifying" products for every imaginable body part. No one can argue with the benefits of a certain amount of youth-enhancing escapism. But at some point, you might want to take a look at what this is getting you. There's no spot in heaven reserved for the best-dressed and -groomed of the population. The feeling that your life has been worthwhile will come from what you do, not how you look.

If you are investing all of your disposable income in yourself, you might be in danger of stagnating—what Erikson considered an unfavorable outcome of the generativity stage—focusing all of your attention on your own personal needs. If it becomes an obsession, you may want to examine your motivation to see what it is you fear about aging and what you're missing out on in terms of giving some of that money and attention to a larger cause.

Learn How to Age Successfully

Many people unfortunately view aging in a negative way and are convinced that with each passing year they become weaker, stupider, and more of a bother to their friends and families. Although our society is getting older, social attitudes toward aging have not kept apace with the population boom, reinforcing these negative stereotypes. However, the reality is that regardless of their health or objective circumstances, people tend to become happier and better adjusted as they get older. Researchers have found that older adults are better able to handle negative emotions and conflict, and rather than dwelling on their limitations, they become adept at focusing on their strengths. They also tend to experience fewer negative emotions because they're able to turn their attention to the positive events in their lives.

It is also true that as we get older, we are increasingly confronted with mortality, but, as Walaskay and I, along with many subsequent researchers have found, those people who age successfully do not spend a great deal of time involved in thinking about death. They are too busy engaging in life, enjoying their daily activities and their families.

Medical researchers have known for decades that even though genetics play an important role in determining how well we age physically, there are a number of ways we can influence the rate of the aging process as it unfolds within our bodies. The key to aging well is activity—physical as well as mental. The normal rate of the aging process in such areas as aerobic capacity (our ability to keep our body's tissues oxygenated while our muscles are at work) is a loss of about 1 percent per year. But if we engage in a regular program of exercise, such as running on a treadmill or an elliptical machine, even for as little as twenty or thirty minutes for three to five days a week (although of course some experts recommend daily exercise), we can cut that rate in half. You don't even have to go that far if you don't want to or don't have the time. Walking instead of driving and taking the stairs instead of the elevator are just two ways to become more physically active within your existing daily schedule.

Physical activity can maintain our bodies; mental activities help to maintain our minds. Most experts who study the aging of intellectual functions recommend that we engage in work and leisure activities that challenge us to solve problems, use our memories, and learn new skills. These activities include using our language skills by doing things such as crossword puzzles, and using our spatial and logic abilities by doing things such as Sudoku. One of the most important keys to keeping our mental functions young is to avoid the trap that many people fall into, which is to believe that they are becoming "senile."

In fact, the phrase people use to describe the memory failures they believe are due to aging is "having a senior moment." Many of us unfortunately have been convinced by the media that senility is an inevitable feature of aging. We hear reports that there are more than five and a half million people in the United States alone who suffer from Alzheimer's disease, and that the number is going to skyrocket as the baby boomers become older. So when we have a memory slip, we conclude that we have now entered the ranks of the millions of mentally incompetent people who will soon be taking over the world.

The truth is that the prevalence of Alzheimer's disease has been grossly exaggerated by the press, who take their cue from an epidemiological study conducted in the early 1980s on the residents of East Boston, Massachusetts. Projections were made from this small and not very representative sample to the entire United States. Despite the fact that subsequent studies estimate that the prevalence of the disease is about half this number, the "five million" (and counting) persists.

Alzheimer's disease is a tragic illness, and when it does strike, it is relentless and devastating. Certainly if you are suffering persistent memory loss, you should be tested, but the chances are small that your memory will deteriorate significantly as a result of the normal aging process and the chances are even smaller that you will develop this disease.

But in addition to giving up on their mental abilities, people who wrongly conclude that they've got Alzheimer's may actually perform more poorly than they would otherwise. Psychologists are finding that the people who believe the stereotypes about aging do worse on memory tests than the people who are resistant to these negative portrayals of aging. Even if a person is not conscious of adhering to the aging stereotypes, the belief that aging is associated with mental decline can become a self-fulfilling prophecy.

Being overwhelmed by negative stereotypes about aging can lead to all kinds of problems, not just a poor memory. As we get older, we are all confronted with certain changes. It's harder to see things up close without reading glasses, we may need people to repeat what they say to us due to changes in our hearing, and we may have trouble getting up the stairs if our knees are a little stiff. When these changes begin to occur, you can either conclude that you're falling apart and will soon be in a nursing home or you can take the changes in stride. The people who minimize the importance of age-related changes and don't get discouraged are the ones who feel better about themselves and will age more successfully in the long run.

In other words, some denial is in many ways the best strategy for coping with the aging process. I don't mean total denial to the point of trying to look and act like a twenty-year-old. The people I've studied who have the highest self-esteem have accepted the fact that they're growing older, but in their everyday lives, they just don't think about it that much. They don't define themselves in terms of their age—they define themselves in terms of the identity they have maintained throughout their lives. They're Sarah, John, Barbara, and William, not "old people" or, worse, "senile." Continuity in your view of who you are can help you resist the labels thrust at you by a society that judges you on the basis of stereotypes of what people are like at different ages.

There are plenty of people who don't fit society's stereotypes of aging. Think about Henri Matisse, the French painter, who in his eighties turned to collages and cutouts when he could no longer handle a brush. Composers such as Verdi and Bruckner produced their greatest masterpieces in middle and later life. If you're feeling limited or constrained by your age, thinking about these role models can be inspiring.

The phrase "use it or lose it" was, to the best of my knowledge, first concocted by the well-known sex researchers William Masters and Virginia Johnson. They were talking about the effect of the aging process on sexuality. Having observed in their lab a number of volunteer subjects of all ages as they engaged in sexual relationships, Masters and Johnson concluded that there was no physical reason for aging people to stop enjoying this aspect of their lives. Instead Masters and Johnson found that the only limitation imposed on an enjoyable sex life was the termination of sexual activity. To keep their sexual organs in the best of health, it was best for people to, as Masters and Johnson famously said, "use it or lose it."

Now this phrase has come to adopt a wider meaning, and we speak in general terms about the need to keep your mind and your body active as you get older. Not only will the mental and physical exercise benefit the way your mind functions, but it will also get you out and about, and you will more likely interact and engage with a variety of people. According to Erikson, it's that involvement with others that will stimulate your development of ego integrity.

Forecast for the Baby Boomers

How will the baby boomers approach aging? At least for the ones who participated in the antiauthority movements of the 1960s, it's a good bet that they will try to redefine the meaning of "old." They will be requesting that rock music be piped into the halls of the nursing homes they eventually occupy. They won't be told they are too old to wear jeans or bikinis. They won't spend their money as wisely as their parents did, and it's unlikely that they'll put as much of it in savings.

Of course, it's risky to generalize, and it can be foolish to try to predict how millions of people will react to a process that we know varies in the way it unfolds for each individual.

It's also likely that the culture of youth and beauty that the baby boomers reified may turn around and catch up with them. The Britney Spearses of the world will continue to emerge as teen idols and potentially displace the baby boomers from the center stage of what is considered cool. To a certain extent, it's already happened.

The baby boomers are thought to be selfish and materialistic, focused on their own needs as they wildly spend money on their expensive habits. However, as we have seen already, the baby boomers grew up at a time when social values such as community service and volunteerism were highly esteemed. In my sample there are a number of people who have taken the high road by becoming involved in causes that extend beyond their own personal interests and needs.

Involvement in social causes or projects for nonprofit agencies such as Habitat for Humanity and the American Cancer Society was common among the sample. These baby boomers donate to humanitarian causes, serve as mentors, chair professional organizations as volunteers, serve on the committees of their churches and synagogues, work for the League of Women Voters, and serve on the chamber of commerce. A number of them were in the peace corps, and many have jobs that are in the education and nonprofit sectors. The exposure that they had to social and political activism seems to have had an enduring impact.

Another myth about the baby boomers is that they lack a strong work ethic; in fact, during college the people in my sample were lowest in industry of all cohorts studied. There are a number of possible reasons for this, including the fact that the 1960s were a time when students did not feel particularly connected with the social values of older generations. For many of the women in the sample, college meant a chance to find a husband, and their education came second to their social life. However, by the time they were in their twenties, both the men and women in the sample were well on their way toward developing their careers and an orientation toward work. As they approached their sixties, the industry scores of the group as a whole were relatively high, and most participants were heavily invested in the desire to contribute to the good of society through their work. Women in particular really shot up in their industry scores, showing a healthy development in their feelings of confidence and competence.

A willingness to work hard, along with a belief in the value of helping others outside their immediate circle, was characteristic of a number of people in the sample, many of whom had acquired national reputations as leaders in their respective fields. It's true that the people in my study were able to benefit from their private school education in order to reach these positions, but considering that many of them started their adult lives as essentially uninvolved in the world of work, their rise to prominence suggests that they earned their accomplishments.

You Can Catch Up—and Then Some

Change is what our lives are about. We undergo day-to-day vacillations in our moods, emotions, and personal qualities. At any one point in time these changes may not be observable, but they do eventually add up. From our knowledge about how to use the appliances in our homes (eventually even the best washing machine breaks down!) to our understanding of world politics, we are constantly adding to our storehouse of skills and knowledge. So if you think that there's no way you can change yourself, consider the fact that you have already changed in many ways from the person you were when you began your life path early in adulthood.

One of my study's most striking findings, a pattern that I saw time and time again, was that a young adulthood marked by uncertainty and doubt did not necessarily predict a middle age of failure and unhappiness. No matter how you started out or where you are now, it is possible for you to get back on track with your original goals and dreams, or to find and define new ones. Don't feel that the steps you take into the future need to follow on a direct path from the ones you took in the past.

You may think that your life is too short to take these corrective actions. Try not to fall into this trap! None of us know how long our lives will be, and if we based our actions on predictions about the time we have left, we would limit ourselves unnecessarily. The people in my study who scored highest on crucial personality scales reflecting ego integrity and generativity were the ones who allowed themselves to take an unlimited view of their future. So you won't live forever, but you might as well take the life you have now by the horns and make those changes you thought were impossible.

If you allow yourself to think of your life in terms of the big picture, you can do more than "catch up." You can propel yourself to new heights of joy and fulfillment. Your life's script is one that you can write any way you want to, starting right now.

Acknowledgments

The Search for Fulfillment is more than a book title for me—the writing of this book represents the fulfillment of decades of studying, writing about, and listening to the stories of my students, colleagues, clients, supervisors, and research participants. Several particular individuals helped me achieve the goal of crystallizing these experiences into book form, which they did with both emotional dedication to the project and a willingness to provide concrete assistance over a period of months, if not years.

Most notable is my agent, Gillian MacKenzie, who had the steadfast belief that this book would provide a new and inspirational message about the fact that anyone can change at any point in life. Her creative ideas and willingness to brainstorm, from the early phases of the book's conceptualization throughout the writing (and beyond), are tremendously appreciated.

I would also like to express my most heartfelt thanks to Carlin Flora for her assistance in editing and shaping my writing to allow me to get across the book's message in as effective and dynamic a way as possible.

At Ballantine Books, Christina Duffy has proven to be as thorough, resourceful, and supportive an editor as any author could hope for. Of course, I am also extremely grateful to Caroline Sutton, who signed the book when she was at Ballantine and guided me through its early phases of development.

The research on which this book is based could not have been conducted without the help of several colleagues who at the time were graduate students in the clinical psychology program at the University of Massachusetts Amherst. Karyn Skultety and Joshua Bringle assisted me in various aspects of data collection, including working very long hours in the lab scanning the Internet for clues as to the whereabouts of my participants. Joel Sneed, who based his dissertation on much of the data from the study presented here, has continued to collaborate with me on the various scientific papers emerging from the project.

I am, of course, indebted to my husband and children for their insights and support throughout the writing of the book. My older daughter, Stacey, with whom I was pregnant when I began my work on the study in the late 1970s, now has her doctorate in psychology and is pursuing a research career studying health and aging. My younger daughter, Jenny, has also chosen to pursue a doctorate in psychology, focusing on the clinical profession. Both of my children, by virtue of their interest in psychology and their wisdom beyond their years, have not hesitated to let me know when I'm being too long-winded or corny or both.

My husband, Richard O'Brien, the only biochemist in the family, is himself a prolific reader and a never-ending source of patience, insight, and wit. I hope I have done justice to the faith that all of you have in my ability to translate my life's work into a form that will be of use to others.

Finally, I would like to express my deep thanks to the 182 participants who shared their personality data with me. I hope I have been able to live up to the trust you put in me to help inspire others with the message that change is always possible.

About the Author

SUSAN KRAUSS WHITBOURNE is one of the first pioneers in the study of adult development and has been leading the field for more than thirty years. She received her doctorate in psychology from Columbia University and is currently a celebrated professor of psychology at the University of Massachusetts Amherst. Whitbourne has received numerous professional recognitions, from the Distinguished Teaching Award and Outstanding Advising Award at the university to the Distinguished Mentorship Award from the American Psychological Association Division of Adult Development and Aging.

Considered the go-to expert on adult development both inside and outside academia, Dr. Whitbourne has been interviewed for and cited in numerous popular psychology articles, including articles for *The New York Times, Newsweek, Redbook,* and *Glamour.* Additionally, her work has been the topic of interviews on the Discovery Health Channel and in an online guide to the PBS series *Discovering Psychology.* A frequent speaker, she has given many invited addresses and public lectures.

Dr. Whitbourne is also a licensed psychologist. Her clinical experience and insights combined with her training as a developmental psychologist give her a unique way of looking at people that informs the ideas she presents to her readers. She lives with her husband in Amherst, Massachusetts.